David Adam was born _____ was Vicar of Danby in North Yorkshire for over 20 years, where he discovered a gift for writing prayers in the Celtic pattern. His first book of these, *The Edge of Glory*, achieved immediate popularity. He has since published several collections of prayers and meditations based on the Celtic tradition. His books have been translated into various languages, including Finnish and German, and have appeared in American editions. Recently David retired from being Vicar of Holy Island, where he had taken many retreats and regularly taught school groups on prayer. He now continues this work and his writing from Waren Mill in Northumberland.

The Road of Life

Reflections on searching and longing

DAVID ADAM

Illustrations by
Monica Capoferri

morehouse

First published in Great Britain in 2004 by
Society for Promoting Christian Knowledge (SPCK)
36 Causton Street, London SW1P 4AU

Morehouse Publishing, P.O. Box 1321, Harrisburg, PA 17105

Morehouse Publishing, The Tower Building, 11 York Road,
London SE1 7NX

Morehouse Publishing is a Continuum imprint.

The publisher and author acknowledge with thanks permission to
reproduce extracts from the following:
A prayer, 'Lord, it is dark', from *Prayers of Life*, by Michel Quoist,
published by Gill & Macmillan Ltd, Hume Avenue, Park West, Dublin 12.

*Every effort has been made to acknowledge fully the sources of material
reproduced in this book. The publisher apologizes for any omissions that
may remain and, if notified, will ensure that full acknowledgements are
made in a subsequent edition.*

Scripture quotations are from the New Revised Standard Version of the
Bible (Anglicized version), copyright © 1989 by the Division of Christian
Education of the National Council of the Churches of Christ in the USA.
Used by permission. All rights reserved.

The stories in this book are all based on real events, but in order to
preserve anonymity the names and some of the details have been changed.

Printed and bound in Great Britain by Bookmarque Ltd, Croydon, Surrey

First edition   1 3 5 7 9 10 8 6 4 2

ISBN 0–8192–2169–4

Cataloguing-in-Publication Data is available from the
Library of Congress

Contents

To Denise,
who shares my journey

Introduction

The invitation to become the vicar of Holy Island came as a surprise. I was working on the North Yorkshire Moors, having three churches and three railway stations in the parish. Denise, my wife, and I thought, as we had completed twenty-three years in this one parish, we would spend the rest of our lives there. We were reasonably settled. Yet somewhere at the back of our minds there was something else saying, 'Move on.'

In the latter part of 1989, the Bishop of Newcastle rang and said he would like to offer me the parish of Holy Island. At first, the idea filled us both with horror. Why move? But we decided we ought at least to go and look at the parish and the vicarage. We knew the Island, though not very well. 'How lucky to go to such a small parish,' said a friend (the village covers less than a square mile and there are only about 150 inhabitants). This friend was an inner-city clergyman who actually had fewer people living in his parish! The bishop told me of the small congregation who met regularly. He also spoke of the Island being a special place, a place of the saints and also one of outstanding natural beauty. We had our doubts and the idea of such a saintly place was daunting. Fortunately, I knew that the Islanders had a reputation of being very down to earth. We came. We looked and we hesitated. We tried to escape the challenge, but it would not let us go. Another friend said, 'It is just the sort of place made for you. You can see God's hand at work.' I only wished that I could see. I asked God to guide me but he gave me no clear directions! It took us three months to make up our minds, another three months to serve our notice and to get rid of twenty-three years of clutter. We arrived just after Easter 1990 to look after, to learn from and to share with 150 people: men, women and children.

We had our suspicions, but no one had mentioned the number of pilgrims to the Island. The pilgrims would come as individuals, in small groups or occasionally three or four thousand at a time. Nearly all these groups expected some input, or at least some guidance on how to cope logistically with 4,000 pilgrims at once. For example, I had to advise them on how long it took to walk the sands and how difficult it could be. They also had to know how long it would take 60-plus buses to leave the island with the threat of an incoming tide. Such large groups had to be told to inform the police of their coming, to bring a St John's Ambulance team with them and to bring their own portaloos! They needed to know how long it took to administer Communion to a large group and how many chalices, patens and assistants it would take. Such information helped to bring many groups down to earth! Then there were school groups, many unplanned, who thought they could just use the building. In a year we would deal with about 7,000 children. On one horrendous day – I should be able to say glorious, because the weather had stopped school groups doing other things – instead of the eighty to ninety we had booked in, we had over nine hundred and fifty children in three hours.

The vicarage would receive endless visitors looking for

hope, healing, help or simply hospitality. Some booked, others arrived on the doorstep. You could not tell if someone was merely curious and fancied seeing into your house or whether they were suicidal. Each needed to be given time and attention and to be treated with discernment. The doorbell, the telephone and the church bell all demanded attention and often at the same time. There was the odd occasion when we had someone needing attention in each of our downstairs rooms and someone waiting across at the church. We averaged about three visitors a day for every day of the year, and that only counts the ones that took over a quarter of an hour of our time.

The rhythm of daily worship would ensure some balance in this hyperactive existence, though some might not think so since we had a minimum of three services a day, not counting any others for school groups or pilgrims. There were odd days when I was in church for over six hours. Fortunately we were able to build up a team of helpers. Still, there was little time to be proactive as we had too much to react to.

There was a great danger of not having time for each other, for ourselves or for the seekers who came to us. Yet this was a greatly rewarding life. We saw the Church alive, exciting and, often, in great numbers. So many people enriched us. As pilgrims shared their journey they often allowed us to share in their insights. We learnt from them new hymns, new modes of worship, deep and meaningful readings, and a great keenness of adventure in the faith. We learnt of humility, perseverance and tremendous courage. Sometimes we were given a material gift, such as when the group from Selkirk brought us a 'Selkirk Bannock' or when the pilgrims from Trondheim brought us St Olaf's head! Fortunately this latter gift was a small plaster cast and not the real thing.

Holy Island has been a place of pilgrimage for over 1,300 years. It is a small island off the Northumbrian coast and near the border with Scotland. The Island can be seen from the A1 when you travel north from Belford and also from the main railway line south of Berwick. As a tidal island the phases of the moon and the tides govern all movements. High tide is never at the same time two days in a row. The movements of residents, pilgrims, fishermen, the wading birds and the vicar are all controlled each day. Twice in every twenty-four hours the Island is cut off by the North Sea and no one can reach us by road.

Bede, who was an early authority on tides, calls the island a demi-isle and writes of it and its tides: 'As the tide ebbs and flows, this place is surrounded twice daily by waves of the sea like an island, and twice, when the sands are dry it becomes again attached to the mainland.'

Walter Scott, in his poem 'Marmion', writes more romantically of tide and pilgrim:

> The tide did now its flood-mark gain,
> And girdled in the Saint's domain:
> For with the ebb and flow its style
> Varies from continent to isle;
> Dry shod o'er the sands, twice every day,
> The pilgrims to the shrine find their way;
> Twice every day, the waves efface
> Of staves and sandall'd feet the trace.
>
> ('Marmion' 2.8)

No one can expect to cross to the Island just when they decide to. Tide tables must be consulted to find out when the way is clear. It is of no use to arrive just after the tide has closed the causeway or if you need a quick exit at high tide. I had to instil this into the minds of pilgrims and visitors and remind them it was the sea they were dealing with. Occasionally I would offer a few extracts from the parish register to those who took the North Sea lightly:

Jan. 8th 1584	old John Stapleton drowned.
Nov. 5th 1641	Samuel Waddell and his son drowned in the Low.
July 28th 1746	Rob. Brown, Clerk of Holy Island drowned.
April 8th 1801	William Macmillan drowned in passing the sands.
Dec. 15th 1802	Alexander Warwick died in crossing the sands.

I have to admit that there have been no deaths on crossing to the Island since the 1950s, though many a car has been ruined by seawater totally covering it.

It is a wonderful sight to see thousands of pilgrims singing as they cross the sands. Large groups of pilgrims, often barefooted, following a person carrying a cross, find this crossing to the Island very moving in itself. Every Good Friday, the Northern Cross Pilgrims meet to carry full size crosses over the sands. Some will have carried these crosses down from Scotland or across England from west to east. The same large crosses are decorated with flowers on Easter Day and brought into the church, which is not big enough to contain all the pilgrims.

The Pilgrims' Way has been used since the seventh century, when pilgrims came in great numbers to the shrine of St Cuthbert. Because of quicksand and the tortuous winding of the River Low, the Pilgrims' Way was clearly marked out. The monks placed cairns at regular intervals, some of which can still be seen. In the 1860s a series of posts were driven into the sand to be a clearer guide for pilgrims and travellers. Still too many people were losing their way. In 1954 a metalled road was provided for cars to cross the sands. It was only in 1965 that this road was completed, with a bridge over the River Low and a refuge box on stilts where anyone caught by the tide can climb into for safety. In 1987, to commemorate the 1,300th anniversary of Cuthbert's death, new poles were erected across the length of the Pilgrims' Way.

The journey to the Island is very like the pilgrimage of life. Sometimes the way is easy, level going and without hindrance. At other times we find our way blocked and we can do nothing about it but wait. No amount of jumping up and down or getting irate will change the situation, unless you are Moses or have the cloak of Elijah! There are times when we must move forward without delay or the opportunity will have gone and the road before us will be closed. Sometimes life is all at sea and then another time a road opens up suddenly before us. At all times we need to accept the wisdom, knowledge and guidance of those who have gone before us. We need to plan our journey and be aware of any hazards we may encounter. Without a doubt we are all travellers in this world, if not pilgrims. We are all on a journey along the road of life.

I believe we all need to find our own 'Holy Island', a place that is special and important to us. We should seek this place until we find it, though I do believe it can be of the heart and carried within us. It will be this quest and awareness that will distinguish a pilgrim from a traveller. Our pilgrim journey is not only measured in miles but takes us into the depths of our being and the mystery of creation. We are not just surface travellers; we are seeking to enter great deeps. We travel with and in God. Actually everyone does, but I am talking of awareness, no matter how tenuous it is. As pilgrims, we are seeking to extend our awareness and our love for God and for all of his creation. The road of life is a journey into love and into God and if we miss out on this we have lost our way.

This is a book about pilgrimage, about the great variety of pilgrims I have met and part of their story. Some pilgrims I have shared a few days with, some I have been with for only a few precious moments. When I write about them I tell only a little of what I see. I have always believed that each pilgrim, each encounter, each person, each creature is unique. No one is dull or unimportant. The closer you get to anyone, or in fact to anything, the richer and more mysterious you find them. The searching and story of any individual are unique to them; they have a long history and cannot be understood in a moment. Everyone must be treated with respect and dignity.

I want to look at pilgrims as mirrors of our own strengths and weaknesses. I want to see them as mirrors in which we recognize familiar reactions and expressions that we have, or have had, at certain stages in our journey through life. Yet at all times we must not forget they are living people, often with concerns of which we know nothing. I do not set them before you to be laughed at or pitied but rather that you may look at yourself more care- fully. We are often angry with people who share the same tendencies and weaknesses that we have ourselves. We find it hard to forgive those that reflect our own weak- nesses when we have difficulty in forgiving ourselves. Come with me and join these pilgrim people. Meet fellow travellers and seekers with similar passions, joys and fears. Learn from their mistakes and their delights. Know that the image they present to us is often our image and that we are all asked to be the image of God.

I want to capture moments, as a camera would capture a moment, for our own education and learning. Later, even a few minutes on, the person may be quite different. You must remember that the people I write about have all moved on and are not frozen into the posture in which I caught them. All are more wonderful, more mysterious and more complex than the snapshot I place before you. For some the very act of pilgrimage and the encounter on Holy Island was a turning point in their lives. For others it may have been just another experience to drop into the box of recollections. Yet, I believe that everyone who comes to the Island leaves something of themselves, and everyone takes away something of the Island with them.

In the same way I believe that the saints, such as Aidan, Cuthbert and Eadfrith, have left us a rich heritage of themselves as well as their works. It is this that makes the Island such a rich place and a good place for pilgrimage. We can walk where the saints have trod. We can pray where they have said their prayers. We can look upon scenery that is almost unchanged since the time of these holy people and let it inspire us too. We can journey down the road of life and be deeply aware of the past, or if we so choose we can walk the same landscape unseeing and unmoved. We may not be able to control where life will take us but we can choose how we react to it. Come and adventure with the pilgrims who sought deeper meanings to the road of life.

> Come on pilgrimage.
> Let us walk together the road of life.
> We will go on well trodden paths,
> and also open us new ways.
> We will seek,
> we will search,
> we will rejoice,
> and perhaps we will sing.

You cannot come as an onlooker,
that leaves you on the outside,
yet still influencing us,
as we influence you.
Come and share your experiences,
your sorrows and your joys.
If your prayer has gone dead,
your God is too small,
your vision too narrow,
Come journey into new depths,
let life be an adventure.

Come and participate,
come and discover –
we will go to strange places,
we may even meet dragons.
But we do not journey alone
we go together along the road
and our God goes with us.

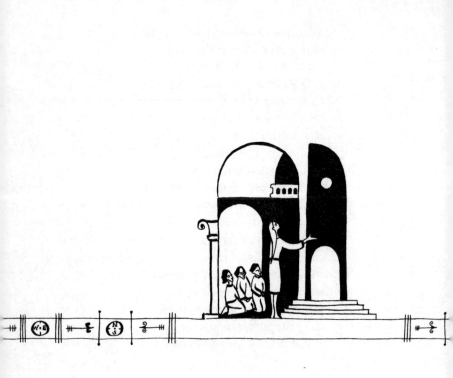

The Lord is Here

It was a typical August day. It was noon and I had already taken three services and spoken to over sixty American visitors. The church was heaving with people. At this moment it felt more like a supermarket than a place of prayer. I just wanted to escape. At the back of the church sat a busload of Saga pilgrims, obviously a little tired. They were trying to eat their packed lunches without being noticed. In the south aisle a very intelligent man was standing by the facsimile of the Lindisfarne Gospels and proclaiming his wisdom. He was speaking in a stage whisper so that all could hear and acknowledge it. In the north aisle a group of children were sitting on the carpet and making merry sounds. Their chortling showed they were very happy to be where they were. There were at least 150 people just wandering around, most looking rather lost. There were three mums with buggies in the main aisle. (I am convinced that people with buggies – or supermarket trolleys – tend to display their genetic descent from Boudicca! Anyone who stands in the road is in danger of being mown down.) Someone stopped me and asked, 'Do you still have services in this church?' When I told him, 'At least three every day,' he refused to believe me, saying, 'No one goes to church that often.' I felt I had had enough for one morning. What can be done with such a madding crowd? With the excuse of lunch, it was time to escape this busy place.

Before I could get to the door, in strode a group of young people. They made straight for the front pews on either side of the main aisle. As there were about twenty of them, they almost filled four pews. After a deep bow to the east, they all knelt except one. This was a pretty young woman who stood with arms raised in prayer. Suddenly, the whole church was silent. The air began to tingle. There was some strange power at work. You could actually feel it. No one in the church dared to move. The children were the first to sense the change and became absolutely still and quiet. The loud speaker ceased from his lecture. The Saga pilgrims stopped eating their sandwiches and bowed their heads. All were being touched by something deep and mysterious. You could actually feel something with your whole being. There was a sense of expectancy in the air. We were waiting for something to happen. After a while, the young woman lowered her arms. The whole group then arose, made a bow and went out. They left a hushed building and people that were aware that something special had just taken place. How long the vibrant silence lasted I could only guess. It must have been at least two or three minutes.

Who were these young folk? What had made them come here and what were they doing in the church? I could not resist following them out and enquiring about their visit. Sadly, I should have been able to guess they were not English. In fact they could not speak English except for one young man. His sentences were slow and thoughtful. 'We are from Slovakia. As Christians, we have a new freedom. To celebrate our new liberty, we sought one of the holiest places we had heard of and came to give thanks to God. Our pilgrimage is one of thanksgiving.'

Needless to say, I was deeply moved by the directness and simplicity of his statements. It was the next sentence that caused me much joy and amusement. 'I hope that we did not disturb anyone.' I could only take his hand and say, 'Thank you. I believe that you have disturbed us all by revealing the presence that is ever with us. God bless you all on your journey.'

I would never see these young people again but what they did that busy August day would remain with me for ever. Without words they had introduced our visitors to the holy and the mysterious. Their faith gave them a confidence, not in themselves but in their God. They rejoiced in his presence and helped others to be more aware of the God in their midst. I am sure they did not need to come to the Island to find God, they knew that God was with them. They did not come to proclaim God, yet their very lives and actions said, 'God is with us.'

Here was I, called to look after a holy place and I was ready to write it off for the day because of the crowds. Was I not in danger of excluding God from the fullness of life, from busyness and human encounter? This group of young folk said strongly, without words, 'God is here. His presence is with us.' They rejoiced in a presence that was part of their daily life. They were not seeking God on the Island, they were here to give thanks that God was with them in their joys and sorrows, in their captivity and in their new-found freedom. Yet some of the visitors to the church that day would remember how these young folk brought God to them. I am sure these young worshippers had no thought of being missionaries. They did not come to preach. Yet, their lives spoke far louder than words. They did not come to talk about God but they did introduce a whole group of people to a presence that day. In many ways these young folk reminded me of the early Celtic saints.

The Celtic saints were said to leave their homes *pere-grini pro Dei amore* or *peregrini pro Christi amore*, that is, as 'pilgrims for the love of God' or 'pilgrims for the love of Christ'. This would distinguish them from those who were just wanderers, or in our terms tourists. The word *peregrini* means wanderers or travellers. Because of their different pattern to the stars, the planets were called 'wandering stars'. For these early Christian travellers it was not wanderlust or the desire to see new places that made them leave their homes and monasteries, it was the call and the love of God. In their journey along the road of life they sought the depth to their own existence and a closer awareness of the presence of God. They would have happily said the words of a modern writer:

> God our pilgrimage impels,
> To cross sea-waste or scale life-fells;
> A further shore,
> One hill brow more,
> Draws on the feet, or arm-plied oars,
> As our soul onward, upward soars.
>   (G. R. D. McLean, 1961, p. 55)

Pilgrimage is often not just a seeking of God but a response to his call. The journey is not only to find God, it is to travel in his presence and to journey deeper into the mystery and wonder of that presence and love. Every seeker is responding to a call to something higher and nobler, or to an emptiness that yearns to be filled. In fact emptiness and boredom are often a call for us to move on and to be changed. We all know there are greater meanings and depths to life and are challenged to come out of our safety and security. We need to recognize that our restlessness is often the call to look in new directions that we may discover the presence and love of God which is about us. How well we should heed the words of St Augustine of Hippo, 'Lord, our hearts are restless until they rest in you.'

Sometimes we have to move out beyond the safe and the secure to become more aware of the mystery of our world. Leaving the familiar and predictable for a while gives us a better chance of moving on in our lives. Dislocation can deepen our awareness. We take our wrists for granted but if we dislocate a wrist we realize just how important it is to us. Dislocation can make us appreciate our home and our way of life. The Celtic saints, by living as strangers in a strange land for Christ's sake, were able to deepen their awareness of the reality that they were citizens of another kingdom. By going away from home they discovered that they were *Hospites mundi*, 'Guests of the world'. This did not mean they did not belong to the world, or that they did not like the world. They often showed a great love for the world. But they acknowledged that, for them, it was a transitory place, a place of perpetual change that was only part of their life. They recognized that they were travellers on the road of life. For pilgrimage to be real it has to be a moving experience! The outer journey is a visible sign that we are being moved and changed in our inner being. More important than the place that we are travelling to is our attitude, our intention and the involvement of our heart.

I had a very holy site, the church on Holy Island, to look after and saw only bustle and crowds. A group of young people came and placed themselves before God! Without words they proclaimed the presence of God in our midst. I did not go for my lunch until I had returned to the church and said the words of Jacob, 'Surely the Lord is in this place and I did not know it.'

There are two Irish sayings that I like: 'It is not by your feet alone you can come to God.' And, 'Your feet will bring you to where your heart is.' Travel for the sake of it can often help you to avoid being a pilgrim. To fill your eyes and your mind with new places and new experiences will not benefit you unless the heart is touched. Here is some advice from medieval Ireland to those that travel to Rome; you could change the destination to any place:

> Going to Rome? Going to Rome?
> It will bring much trouble, little gain.
> Your long journey could be in vain.
> The King you seek, will only appear
> If in your heart you brought him here.

I have met 'pilgrims' who are wearied with their journey and long for the comfort and familiarity of home. One little Northern lad expressed it well, 'What's here? There's not even a chip shop!' Some are not at home anywhere and so pilgrimage often leaves them unchanged. I see pilgrims reflecting the feeling of Matthew Arnold in his poem 'The Grand Chartreuse',

> Wandering between two worlds, one dead,
> The other powerless to be born
> With nowhere yet to rest my head.

One man reflected this when he asked if he could stay for our evening service. He said, 'I will sit right at the back, I do not want to be involved.' I could not say to him this was not possible. If he was not involved he could not possibly understand what we were doing. We were placing our hearts before our God. We were offering our whole being. The words might sound dull and boring to an outsider but for us this was a love affair. You cannot really understand a love affair if you have no involvement. Yet God is gracious; perhaps God would touch this man through our words and actions. If the heart is not involved in the journey it will benefit us little. I believe we have dual citizenship: we belong to two worlds and should enjoy them both. Too often Christians give the impression you should turn your back on this God-given world. God has created this world and loves it. If we despise the creation and reject it how can we learn to love the Creator? Take to heart the words of St Ignatius Loyola:

> God freely created us so that we might know, love and serve him in this life and be happy with him for ever. God's purpose in creating us is to draw forth from us a response of love and service here on earth, so that we may obtain our goal of everlasting happiness with him in heaven.
>
> All things in this world are gifts of God, created for us, to be the means by which we can come to know him better, love him more surely and serve him more faithfully.
>
> As a result, we ought to appreciate and use these gifts of God insofar as they help us towards our goal of loving service and union with God. But insofar as any created things hinder our progress toward our goal, we ought to let them go.
>
> (*The Spiritual Exercises*,
> The Institute of Jesuit Sources, 1978, p. 23)

In order that we may live well, we need to be sure of our relationship with this world and the next. The young folk who gave silent thanks to God did so for the new freedom that they had in this world. No doubt that freedom reflected their longing for the glorious freedom of the children of God.

Teilhard de Chardin outlines the dangers of a divided heart and mind if we do not love God and the world aright. He suggests that most Christians are in danger of becoming 'distorted, disgusted, or divided'. We become distorted when we deny our taste for the tangible world and make ourselves look at purely religious objects. To do this we need to banish so much of the beauty and splendour that is about us. In denying our natural love for the world we distort the truth about ourselves and our God. The disgusted decide that the world is too wonderful to deny and they turn their backs on God, like the man who went away sorrowing because he had too many riches. They seek to live thoroughly human lives without recourse to any higher being. Yet they know in themselves that there is more to this world and in themselves than they are acknowledging. To deny all mystery and wonder is to diminish ourselves and our horizons. The third group is the most common and that is the divided. They give up any attempt of making sense of the situation; they never belong wholly to God or wholly to things. Such people often live by double standards and are seen as insincere.

We can all experience this division in ourselves at times. There are many times in our lives when we are not wholly there, when we are not giving our attention or ourselves. To travel in body but not in spirit is to be a tourist but not a pilgrim. Yet even a tourist needs to be there; Annie Dillard says, 'Beauty and grace are performed whether or not we will sense them. The least we can do is try to be there'. Sadly, divided people are rarely present wherever they are. To travel in body but not in heart cannot bring us peace or satisfaction. Though we must not forget that the love of God seeks to break in at all times. God offers himself to us whether we are aware of it or not.

Many of the Christians who want to go on pilgrimage have been detained for a while from their journey. Christians under obligation to work, state or family may not have the freedom of movement they would like. Lack of resources or courage can prevent the beginning of pilgrimage, at other times it can be direct opposition or an anti-Christian environment. Some may even be in prison. Then, like many that have gone before them, they have to make a pilgrimage of the heart. I often suggest to people that they become 'armchair pilgrims'. When we are detained in body we are still free at heart. One prisoner said to me, 'Though my body is in prison my heart is free.' We have a freedom that no one can take from us, we are God's people and he is with us. Nothing can separate us from God or his love. We need to learn to rest in that love wherever we are, to abide in him and know that he abides in us. Then we will know that God is with us wherever the road of life takes us.

I believe that we rarely discover that the world is a holy place until we have found one holy place. Once we find one holy place there is a chance for all to become holy. Sometimes we can choose a holy place and set our sights on going there one day. We can find out as much as we can about that place and its saints. We can have pictures and icons and films about it. If we do this we need to be aware of the danger of fantasy. It is better to discover that the place where you are is holy or at least has the potential for holiness. Let God enter your heart and the place where you are. If you feel that God is far off, remember feelings are liars. 'In him we live and move and have our being.' You are in the presence of God no matter where you are. You are in the heart of God and God seeks to dwell in your heart. Holiness comes with the territory, for the earth is the Lord's and all that is in it. You belong to God and in a wonderful way, God belongs to you.

There is a lovely legend telling of God after the Fall asking his angels where he should hide. Because man had hidden from God, God will now become hidden. A bright little angel said, 'Hide in the heaven.' 'O, no,' said God, 'for humans will always aspire to higher things and they will find me there.' A second glowing angel said, 'Well then, hide in the deep.' Again God replied, 'Human life is full of many depths and they will surely plumb the depths and find me.' The third angel had been biding his time and felt he was now on safe ground. 'Why not hide in the human heart?' God smiled at the angel and decided to do just that. God said, 'I will hide in the human heart and I am sure they will not ever seek me there.' If God is hidden from your sight, you can still find him in your heart. Learn what the Psalmist means when he makes God say, 'Be still, and know that I am God.' The young people from Slovakia travelled deeper into the heart of God while carrying God in their hearts.

If possible, get someone to teach you how to be still before God. It sounds so easy, yet it is fraught with difficulties. There are as many, if not more, dangers on the journey within as there are on any outward journey. At the very start of the journey there should be a notice saying 'Here be dragons'. To learn to meditate or to contemplate the Presence we should normally have a guide. Books can be of great help, as can music and the spoken word, but nothing can replace the careful guidance of someone who is already experienced in these matters. When we set out on any journey it is important that we know we are on the right road. The surest way to keep on the right road is to travel with someone who has been down that way before us. This is true of the journey within as well as any other. Yet in some ways, because each one of us is so unique, we need to make the road as we go: our journey inwards is where no one has been before.

We need to see life and its journey as a great adventure and rejoice in its newness and mystery each day.

After my advising caution, do not be put off. Living in the awareness of the presence of God is so life-enriching. I often start my time of meditation with these words, which are attributed to St Columba:

> Alone with none but thee, my God,
> I journey on my way;
> What need I fear if thou art near,
> O King of night and day?
> More safe I am within thy hand,
> Than if a host did round me stand.

Travel in heart to meet your God, knowing that God is there waiting for you. Pilgrimage of the heart is something we can all practise every day.

There are pilgrims who are fortunate enough to travel both in body and spirit and to come to some holy place. When such pilgrims left home they were not always sure what they would find but they felt in their heart that he would find them and be there. The young pilgrims from Slovakia were not seeking God for they knew him. They were choosing a special place in which to give thanks to him for a new stage in their lives. They were rejoicing that the God of their heart was the God of the whole world and that he reveals himself through special places.

Exercises

1 Pray:

> Kindle in our hearts, O God, we pray
> The flame of love that is never extinguished,
> May it burn in us and give light to others
> May we shine for ever in your presence
> And reflect the light of your glory
> Which disperses the darkness that is about us:
> Through him who is the Light of the World
> Jesus Christ our Lord and Saviour. Amen

2 Practise being aware of the presence. Remind yourself
  that God is with you, whoever you are. Try to do this
  with as few words as possible. Learn just to be there,
  offering yourself to God as he offers himself to you.

3 The 5p Exercise
  One of the ways I use to centre my heart and my whole
  being on God is the 5p exercise. To actually make the
  space and desire God is to begin a pilgrimage. It is to
  turn to God and wait upon him who waits for us. It is
  a 5p exercise because each part of the exercise begins
  with the letter P.

Pause, Presence, Picture, Ponder, Praise.

Pause It is important to come with an undivided
mind. Stop your activity and your need to be busy. Take
time out from your schedule. Be still and quiet and
place yourself in the peace of God. Let the stillness
begin with your body. Relax. Check your feet, hands,
neck for signs of tension. Can you really sit still? Sometimes I purposely tense up my hands, feet and face,

screwing them all up until they almost hurt and then relax them. This helps me to know it is within my power to tense up or to relax. It is within your power to relax, so let go. Let your breathing be deep and comfortable. For a while just watch each breath and enjoy its rhythm. Now relax your mind – this is always harder. Get rid of the angst and the clutter for a while at least. I do not believe you can empty your mind, it has far too much in it to do that. Instead drop into your mind calming thoughts. Know that peace and stillness are offered to you, that God offers himself to you. You may like to repeat the word 'peace' or simply say 'Lord God' each time the mind wants to wander, and so keep the mind in check. I often begin by gently saying:

Come my Lord, my Light, my Way.
Come my Lord, my Light,
Come my Lord,
My Lord.

Though I know God is with me, this helps me to relax into the Presence that is always there.

Presence　　We have entered the stillness to free us that we may give ourselves to God. It is important at this stage to seek to give our self to him. We may have come for another purpose, for peace, for love, for healing. God knows our needs. Before seeking a gift let us seek God: put the Presence before presents. Give your attention to God as you would a friend. Acknowledge his presence. Say, 'Lord you are . . . Lord you are here . . . You are with me . . . You have called me . . . You have asked me to come to you. Lord you are here and I come to you.' It is good to stay in the seeking of God's awareness as long as you can. Remember God is there whatever your feelings. Sometimes all we can say is 'I know you are there in the darkness. I cannot see you or feel you, but I place myself before you.'

Picture   Images are important. This is using our imagination but not imagining, rather in creating important images that will be signs and guides to us. I often choose an image from a song or a hymn, sometimes from an event in the world that reveals the working of God to me. I daily use a passage of Scripture, for here are tested images. For this reason I prefer to choose the Scripture before I start the exercise. Can I suggest you quietly read Exodus 33.12–17.

Picture Moses and the Israelites. They have escaped Pharaoh and are settling into their newfound freedom. They are living in the desert like Bedouin, they have their own kind of security and comfort. This is far better than being slaves in Egypt. They have been here for a year and are beginning to enjoy it. By now, they are familiar with the area around Mount Sinai and are learning the laws of God. God asks Moses to move and to take the people forward to the Promised Land. If they are to enter the Promised Land they will have to leave this place and comfort for the deeper desert and the unknown. Moses is not too sure. To leave security and comfort and take great risks for a promise is asking a lot. Will the people be willing to go with him? Like many, Moses is willing to do God's will but he is not sure what God's will is. He is not sure where God wants him to go. God does not offer him a map: he does not even offer a guide. He offers himself. He reminds Moses that he is ever present and rest is found in him: 'I myself will go with you, and I will give you rest.' The reaction of Moses is wonderfully human: 'If you were not going, do not even think of asking us to leave this place.' God then assures Moses of his abiding presence and that he will go with the Israelites.

Try and picture this scene of Moses at prayer. See him struggling as any human would with the feeling that it is time to move. Be aware of his anxiety and fear of the unknown. He has no certainties. He is not sure of the people's reaction. Will they follow him? Neither is he sure of the journey he should take. In his life there are no securities except that God is with him and will be with him wherever he goes.

Ponder How often do we let comfort and security prevent us from moving on? Most of us prefer the familiar and the safe. Do we see living in the Presence as a call to adventure, to be a pilgrim for the love of God?

Are there signs of unrest, boredom or frustration in your life and can you view them as a call to move on or at least to change your present way of life? How will you know what God wants of you if you do not spend time talking to him and waiting upon him?

Sometimes the impulse for movement is totally outside ourselves. If our work comes to an end or a loved one leaves us, if we need to move house or alter what we are doing we are being compelled to change. There are times when we do not seek the desert yet we find ourselves in it, or the desert within us. Then we need to know we are not alone. We need to know the abiding presence and love of God.

Praise Rejoice that 'we dwell in him and he in us': that God never leaves us nor forsakes us. You might like to repeat the words attributed to St Columba:

> Alone with none but thee, my God,
> I journey on my way;
> What need I fear if thou art near,
> O King of night and day?
> More safe I am within thy hand,
> Than if a host did round me stand.

Or end with the words of the hymn:

> Guide me, O thou great Redeemer,
> pilgrim through this barren land;
> I am weak, but thou art mighty;
> hold me with thy powerful hand:
> bread of heaven,
> feed me now and evermore.
>
> Open now the crystal fountain
> whence the healing stream doth flow;
> let the fiery cloudy pillar
> lead me all my journey through:
> strong deliverer
> be thou still my strength and shield.
>
> When I tread the verge of Jordan,
> bid my anxious fears subside,
> death of death, and hell's destruction,
> land me safe on Canaan's side:
> songs and praises
> I will ever give to thee.

(W. Williams, 1717–91; Welsh,
translated P. and W. Williams)

4 Know that God seeks your love and offer yourself to
  him throughout the day.

> Lord:
> How do I love thee? Let me count the ways.
> I love thee to the depth and breadth and height
> my soul can reach, when feeling out of sight
> for the ends of being and of ideal grace.
> I love thee to the level of every day's
> most quiet need, by sun and candlelight.
> I love thee freely as men strive for right;
> I love thee purely, as they turn from praise.
> I love thee with a passion put to use
> in my old griefs, and with my childhood faith.
> I love thee with a love I seemed to lose
> with my lost saints – I love thee with the breath,
> smiles, tears, of all my life!
> And, God, if thou dost choose
> I shall love thee better after death.
>
>   (Elizabeth Barrett Browning, adapted in
>   *The SPCK Book of Christian Prayer*, 1995, p. 61)

> Eternal God, the light of the minds that know you,
> The joy of the hearts that love you,
> The strength of the wills that serve you;
> Grant us so to serve you that we may truly love you,
> So to love you that we may freely serve you,
> To the glory of your holy name.
>
>   (Fifth-century Gelasian Sacramentary)

Occupied Territory

I first saw him as I was returning to the Island. It had been a busy morning for me, having taken two services, and attended a two-and-a-half-hour meeting ten miles from home. I was on my way for a quick lunch before speaking to a school group. He was plodding along the road and looked as if he was bent double. On his back was one of the largest rucksacks I have ever seen. It looked as if he was carrying all of his possessions with him. In this bowed position he reminded me of Atlas, weighed down with the world upon his back. He looked weary but as he was almost on the Island I did not stop to offer him a lift. It would have taken longer to have got him and his belongings in and out of the car, than it would for him to walk the last few hundred yards.

The next time I met him, though I did not recognize him without his burden, was at the evening service. This was a simple service with a good deal of quietness. During the service his mobile phone rang and he found some difficulty in switching it off. As soon as the service ended he rushed out to see who had called him. He was waiting for me at the church door and apologized for the interruption. He explained he was expecting an important call and had been reluctant to switch the phone off. By now my first impressions were of a man carrying a heavy load and who was unwilling to switch the phone off. He asked if I could spare him a couple of hours. This, as always, caused me to panic a little, two hours is a lot out of any day. I suggested we met for about three-quarters of an hour the next morning and then we could meet again if it proved that our meeting was useful.

The next morning was one of great beauty. The sun rose golden out of a tranquil sea, the seals were singing and the terns flying and calling overhead. My new friend attended the two morning services; this time the mobile phone was silent. At 9.30 am prompt my doorbell rang. He was on the step with a large carrier bag. Once inside, he explained he was on a sabbatical, taking time off from work, and he was doing some research. In the next few minutes I discovered he was also a clergyman from a very busy parish; he needed rest and refreshment. He told me how the bishop had insisted that he had this three-month break and during that time he could write something on Celtic Christians and their approach to prayer. I suggested that I rang his bishop to tell him this was hardly a sabbatical! It soon came to light that he was visiting Iona, Lindisfarne and Celtic sites in Scotland and Ireland, travelling by foot as well as public transport. Because one or two important things were happening in the parish he was keeping in contact with the churchwardens and a friend. He planned to spend most of his time on the Island studying in the library. When I asked him what he hoped to do most of all on the Island his reply was, 'To relax.' Unkindly, my unspoken thoughts were, 'Fat chance!'

Out of his bag came a laptop and a tape recorder. He asked if he could record our conversation and refer to some notes on his laptop. I said I did not mind, as I was quite used to such an approach. He was very tense in his questioning and kept looking at his watch. Almost at the end of our time, the mobile rang from his carrier bag. One of the churchwardens was informing him of some crisis within the parish. If our time had been reasonably restful, he was no longer at peace. He apologized and said he would have to go and make a few phone calls.

I did not see him again until the evening service. He looked very strained and tired. I could not help feeling I needed to give him more attention. He would only be on the Island another two whole days. After the service I suggested he might like to go for a walk, either after his evening meal or in the morning. He said he could not do it, for something of consequence had cropped up and he would have to leave the Island as early as possible. He was going back to his parish for a couple of days before going off to Ireland. He was grateful for our time together and hoped I might like to read his dissertation on the Celts, when it was finished. I again suggested, if he was to leave the following day, he might enjoy a little tour of the Island after his evening meal, especially as he had not really seen anything of it. Once again he politely declined the offer, as he was too busy. The matter that had cropped up would demand all his time and attention.

As he left I felt sorrow for this caring individual. He was very heavily burdened, unable to switch off and in great need of rest and relaxation. The first image, not a kind one, that came to my mind as I walked across to the vicarage was from *The Little Prince*:

'I know a planet where there is a certain red-faced gentleman. He has never smelled a flower. He has never looked at a star. He has never loved anyone. He has never done anything in his life but add up figures. And all day he says over and over, just like you, "I am busy with matters of consequence!" That makes him swell with pride.'

'But he is not a man – he is a mushroom!'

'A what?'

'A mushroom!'

(Saint-Exupéry, 1962, p. 31)

I felt guilty for thinking in this way but even more guilty for I knew that I was often like this man. Even today I had worked from 7 am until 6.30 pm with little room for anything, except what was in my diary. It was time to stop!

The modern training of clergy has many built-in dangers. I often talk to men and women who are in training. They have a full-time job, a home to look after, a local parish church, which they are involved in, and yet they are expected to spend a night a week or more at a lecture, hours in study and to produce an essay every month. Added to this they have a summer school to attend and quarterly weekend courses. Some have to travel straight from work to their lecture, which can be thirty-plus miles from home. I know they need training but we are often in danger of training people who are justified by their works. We are making our clergy hyperactive and then wonder why so many of them come a cropper. So often the strain of training is passed on to their homes and their parishes. People are encouraged to measure life by what they have done and not for who they are. We, who minister, need to offer more stillness and peace to our people. How can we preach peace and the grace of God if we are stressed and strained? How can we offer healing to others if we are so sick ourselves? We need to be able to be present in the present and not to be distracted by the past or the future. We should be able to encourage people to enjoy who they are and where they are. Rilke, in his *Letters on Cézanne*, wrote, 'One lives so badly, because one always comes into the present distracted'.

The sign that we all could often display is 'No room at the inn'. We are often preoccupied and that means we do not have room for anything else, including prayer and God. We fill our diaries and our agendas and feel that this justifies our existence, when in reality it often prevents us from experiencing true meetings and encounters.

One of the things that happens in the holiday season is the double booking of a hotel or a bed-and-breakfast. People arrive expecting a meal and a room, to discover that there is no room at all. The room that they had hoped for is fully occupied. It is terrible for a family to have to drive around and find only 'No vacancy' notices. Often the new cannot enter our lives for we are full of the old. We are unable to give ourselves to someone because our minds and our diaries are full.

I wanted to tape a programme on the television but all my tapes were full. I wanted what was on them and I also wanted to record. I made the choice and missed the programme. I knew that no two programmes can occupy the same piece of videotape at the same time. It is a law of nature that no two things can occupy the same space at the same time. This is as true of our minds and our hearts as it is the rest of the world. Unless we make space in our day and our lives, we become overrun as a garden does with weeds.

When going on holiday we are often restricted as to how much we can carry. Many a holiday limits you to one case weighing only so many kilos. What will you take? Camera, CD player and CDs, binoculars, a few books in case it rains, writing material, a first-aid kit, all sorts of toiletries? That is before you come to the essentials! By the time you add your swimming gear, walking shoes, a large jumper, the case will be refusing to take any more. Once the case is full nothing else will go in, and this is the same with humans. No two things can occupy the same space at the same time. You will have to make a choice. Are you sure that you are allowing the right things to fill your time and your life? Is there any space for the new?

Jesus told a story that illustrates the need to make space in our lives. It is Luke 14.15–24. There was once a man who invited people to his party. He sent out the invitations long before, so that they would know the date and keep it free. Then when the day came he sent out reminders saying, 'Come, for all things are now ready.' And guess what? All those invited were preoccupied. They had filled their diaries and their days. So, they excused themselves. They were polite about it, but they did not come. The frightening thing is, those who excuse themselves exclude themselves.

Listen to the excuses: 'I have bought a field. I will be occupied looking at it, sorry I cannot come.'

'I have bought some oxen and I will be occupied testing them, sorry I cannot come.'

'I have married a wife, she will keep me occupied, sorry I cannot come.'

When this story was told the hearers were meant to laugh at the excuses. Who would buy a house or a field without checking it out? Anyhow, now that it is bought, it will not run away. This is someone excusing and excluding himself due to his own priorities. Who would buy oxen, or a car, without making sure they would pass the test? This man preferred being out with the oxen and so excused and excluded himself. The third had a good excuse, 'I am married, so I cannot come.' Remember this was a world of male dominance. Maybe it was a time of great romance but he made his choice. In excusing himself he excluded himself. All of these were too occupied to come before the presence of the man who invited them. Those who laughed at the excuses must now look to themselves. Our Lord and King invites us to spend time in his presence. We would be enriched by spending some of each day coming before him. Well, we would if we were not too busy.

We would enjoy relaxing with our God, if we did not have such agendas.

Many of us are carrying heavy loads: we are burdened like Atlas. Some of us actually look as if we have the world on our shoulders, bowed down with its weights and cares, or even just a little piece of it. There are so many weary people in the world, so many who feel overladen. Yet so few accept the invitation, 'Come unto me all who are heavy burdened and I will refresh you'. We decide we do not have enough time to spend in quiet before our God. We go rushing around, trying to act like God, and often in ever-decreasing circles with diminishing resources. We need to learn to take time out, to make spaces in our diaries and in our days for our God. I believe we will not really make time for God, unless we are making time for our own families and loved ones. It is often the case that 'As much as you did it to the least of these you did it to me.' Learn to give your attention to those you live with, give them time and your undivided self. Then you will learn how to give yourself to God.

I caught myself trying to read some notes while answering a phone call; neither was getting my undivided attention. If I live like this, I should not get cross with the people who do not turn the television off when I have come to talk with them. So much in our world shouts for attention that we have to make definite decisions about what we are able to give ourselves to. So often the mind is encouraged to try and keep a three-ringed circus going rather than stop and give our attention to one thing.

It is hard to pray if so much activity is going on in our mind. The mind loves to roam about and keep itself occupied. There is a lovely poem on this subject from tenth-century Ireland, called 'Wandering Thoughts':

> Shame on my thoughts,
> How they stray:
> They'll bring me trouble
> On Judgement Day.
>
> During the Psalms they are off
> On a path not right
> Running, misbehaving, distracted
> All in God's sight.
>
> Seeking out wild parties
> With loose women in mind
> Through woods and cities
> Swifter than the wind.
>
> A moment with great beauty
> And loveliness on high
> The next with shameful acts
> I tell you truly, it is no lie.
>
> With no boat or transport
> They can cross every sea,
> Around earth and heaven
> Then return back to me.

They race without wisdom
Forever they do roam,
After such foolishness
They are suddenly home.

If you seek to bind them
Or shackle their feet,
They refuse to be held
Or cease to be fleet.

Sword will not tame them
Neither the strong whip.
Like an eel they slither
And slide from my grip.

No lock, prison nor chain
Will them a moment detain.
No sea, nor strong fortress
Their journeying refrain.

O Beloved, chaste Christ,
To whom all eyes are clear
May your seven-fold Spirit
Check them. Keep them here.

God of the elements
Come rule my will
That you may be my love
And I do your will.

That I may reach Christ
And his holy company.
They are not fickle, unsteady,
Not as the likes of me.

(Tenth-century Irish)

Learn to quieten your mind, and to make spaces in each day, or you will also be forever carrying a heavy load.

Exercises

1 Make a checklist over your waking day. See what occupies you and your time. What, if anything, gets your undivided attention? How much time do you give to your loved ones – making sure you do it? How much time do you spend in quiet before your God?

   Most of us find we spend more time being distracted by television than attracted by God. Is God really among your priorities? Have you a fixed time when you come before God?

2 Unwind. Spend some time each day definitely relaxing. It is good to sit quietly with some music – or to enter into silence. Think of yourself like a coiled spring, wound up and uptight and seek to let this be a time of uncoiling. Think of yourself in a beautiful place, in the sun. Perhaps by a lakeside where the waves are gently lapping. There is no need to do anything. Let go of all tension, take time out. It is amazing how invigorating this can be. Give the body and the mind some time off. Make sure you are comfortable and that each part of your body is at ease. Check your neck, your face, your hands, your stomach, your whole body for signs of tension. There is no need to do anything. Rest in the presence of God as you would in the sunshine. Sometimes when my mind wants to wander I bring it in check with a prayer of affirmation:

God I rest in you:
You are here with me.

God I rest in you:
You are here in the stillness.

God I rest in you:
You are with me always.

God you are with me.
Grant me your peace.

3 Put your trust in God by meditating on Psalm 46.

Verses 1–3. These verses affirm that God is with us, and is our refuge and strength. When the world is rushing around, the very foundations trembling, amid storm and tempest God is with us. He is our stronghold. Often we are afraid to let go because we think that all needs to be done in our strength alone. Rejoice with the psalmist in the presence and in the power of God. Take your time – affirm that God is with you.

Verses 4–7. Jerusalem is on the top of a rocky hill so no river can flow up into it. But just outside the eastern wall there is a natural spring, which they called 'Gihon', which means 'gusher'. The people of Jerusalem looked upon Gihon as a gift from God, a sign of God's grace. When Hezekiah was king he made sure the waters of Gihon ran into the city through an underground tunnel. We need to let the grace of God work in our lives to accept the gift of his presence and his love. It is good to start the day by knowing that God is in the midst of us and that God will help us at the break of each day. Though kingdoms and nations tremble, affirm: 'The Lord of hosts is with us; the God of Jacob is our refuge.'

Verses 8–11. You may like to think upon God's power, the mightiness of his works, or of his desire for peace in the world and in your heart. Heed the words 'Be still, and know that I am God.' Rest in his presence. Be still and know God is with you. Rest and know that God is Almighty. At this point I like to say:

> I weave a silence on to my lips
> I weave a silence into my mind
> I weave a silence within my heart
> I close my ears to distractions
> I close my eyes to attractions
> I close my heart to temptations
>
> Calm me, O Lord, as you calmed the storm
> Still me, O Lord and keep me from harm
> Let all the tumult within me cease
> Enfold me Lord in your peace.

(Adam, 1985, p. 7)

Now let it happen – rest in God and know that God is in you.

4 Throughout the day take little breaks from activity and affirm: 'The Lord of hosts is with us'. I like to simply say 'God is here.' Spend a little time enjoying that reality. I can promise your work and your life will be better for it. Think on the words 'Be still, and know that I am God.' Take mini-rests in his presence, his power and his peace, know that God is with you. You may like to hear our Lord saying to you: 'Come to me, all you that are weary and are carrying heavy burdens, and I will give you rest.'

How Awesome is this Place

A young man who had been taught briefly by my wife Denise, in the infant school, came to the Island to see us. He was among those youngsters who were forever venturing and was often quite naughty. He was from a non-churchgoing family and did not attend church. Most of the time he lived quite a tough existence, though I am sure it was lively and adventurous. As he lived on the North Yorkshire Moors, we had not seen him for over twelve years. One day he found himself coming past the Island and he decided to call. Because he was now a young man he had to remind us who he was. Denise was delighted to see him, as she always enjoys contact with former pupils. After telling us of how he had progressed, he announced that he had become a Christian and what a difference it had made to everything in his life. He now saw the whole world in a new light. That was exciting enough, but to walk around the Island and visit the church with him was a treat. 'It is awesome, absolutely awesome,' he kept saying as he stood looking at the scenery in wonder. He reacted the same in the church when he heard of the lives of St Aidan and St Cuthbert, 'Awesome, absolutely awesome.' His vocabulary was never particularly large but he expressed his feelings well. He was awake to the beauty and the wonder of the world like few people I have met. I did not know whether he had heard of Jacob's dream and his reaction of 'How awesome is this place!' (Genesis 28.10–19, especially verse 17), but he was living with much the same experience.

In a few moments this young man had made me look at my surroundings with greater respect and awe. It was a delight to be with someone so enthusiastic and alive. His joy for living was quite infectious. He was interested in all that was around him and yet seemed able to give his undivided attention to whatever was at hand. Here was someone that enjoyed the world and rejoiced in its Creator. You could almost say he was shining with his joy. This was so different from the grey and weary faces that so often confront us all in our daily living.

After he left, I wrote the following in my diary:

Most people have become too familiar with the mysteries that are about them and the wonder of their own being. There is a great danger in taking the world, ourselves or others for granted. Many no longer see or seek out the beauty and the wonder of creation. They have ceased to thrill at the dawn, at new leaves on trees or the blackbird's song. No longer do they stoop to enjoy the glory that is revealed in a flower or a butterfly, to discover the intricacy and splendour of a wing. It is amazing how so many adults fill their lives with triviality and worry over mere nothings when the glory of the world waits to speak to them.

There is nothing free from mystery if you look deep enough or long enough. This mystery is almost the only way God can speak to us. If we close our eyes to the mysteries about us how can we hope to begin to perceive the great mystery of God? This great mystery is ever present in all that we call earthly or secular. If our eyes were opened we would bow in awe before our Creator. Life takes place within the setting of a great miracle and we can derive endless delight from the contemplation of it. Every thing that is, is holy. Once this is discovered, the whole world is filled with glory. But most of us need to find one holy place before all can be seen as holy. We need to find one special place of the Presence, of rest and peace before we can share this with others and discover that the Presence is with us always. If our attitude to the world is wrong, our attitude to God will also be wrong. If we do not see the beauty and wonder of the world around us, how can we hope to behold the beauty of its Creator?

Against this entry I wrote a quotation from *The Brothers Karamazov* by Dostoevsky:

Love all of God's creation – the whole of it – every grain of sand. Love every leaf, every ray of God's light. Love the animals, love the plants, love everything. If you love each thing you will perceive the mystery of God in all. Once you perceive this, you will begin to comprehend it better every day, and you will come at last to love the whole world with an all-embracing love . . .

Brothers, love is a great teacher; but we must learn how to acquire it, for it is got with difficulty. We buy it dearly, slowly and with much labour. Everyone can love occasionally – even the wicked can do that; but we must love not for a moment but for ever.

The young man was with us only a short afternoon but he left us feeling how rich and wonderful is our world and how fortunate we are to be part of it. He was overawed by the holiness of the place where we lived and worked. It would be far too easy for us to forget this and take it all for granted. Albert Einstein said: 'Whoever is devoid of the capacity of wonder, whoever remains unmoved, whoever cannot contemplate or know the deep shudder of the soul in enchantment, might just as well be dead for he has already closed his eyes upon life' (quoted in Mayne, 1995, p. 109).

I have enjoyed helping groups to give more attention to their surroundings: to open their eyes wide and to look closely at the world about them. To do this I ask them to bring a camera, it does not need to have a film in it. I want them to use the camera as a means of focusing on something, concentrating on one thing only. I ask them to find a single flower or a shell and see if they can focus on it and its structure and beauty. A camera is very useful to help you to focus on one thing, it is a good instrument to help you to concentrate your gaze. (Though I must admit, with some groups devoid of cameras, we have looked through the cardboard tubes from toilet rolls!) In the same way I still thrill at the different vision of the world that is obtainable through a microscope or a telescope. As G. K. Chesterton said, 'Is ditchwater dull? Naturalists with microscopes have told me that it teems with quiet fun.'

If you look at anything closely it will reveal new wonders to you. Wonder is revealed in all things; nothing is common or ordinary, all are filled with power and light. If we do not know this it is because we have not looked close enough or long enough. Those who have closed their eyes, their mind and heart miss the splendour and the wonder of the world. The world is not there only to be classified or measured or even possessed, it is there to be wondered at and to lead us to marvel at its creation, and its Creator. Thomas Carlyle said that 'worship is transcendent wonder'. Wonder is often our first encounter with 'the other', with something vibrant that is beyond classification. It is when we are attracted by wonder that we stand, or kneel, in awe. Wonder opens to us the other and so prepares us to move towards the great Other who is God. It was the wonder of the burning bush that led Moses to holy ground and the abiding presence of God. In this way wonder often gives birth to prayer, to praise, to adoration. The way to the holy is through what we call the ordinary; the way to God is through his creation.

The early Celtic Christians talked of the 'Primary Scriptures'. The New Testament is full of the Good News, but it cannot be understood fully if we do not understand the Old Testament. In its turn the Old Testament cannot be understood fully unless we read the Primary Scriptures. The Primary Scriptures are the world and our own being. The sad thing about much modern education is that it has taught us to read but left us illiterate when it comes to reading the world about us. If we go through a world where we have closed our eyes to wonder, where we have become insensitive to beauty, all around us becomes dull, boring and empty. If we are insensitive to each other, how can we hope to be sensitive to the great Other who is God? I believe that people who have not learnt to give their attention to each other and the world cannot give their attention to God. The world is a great teacher and offers us a joyful entry into the presence of God. Teilhard de Chardin, in that wonderful book *Le Milieu Divin*, says:

. . . we have only had to go a little beyond the
frontier of sensible appearances in order to see the
divine welling up and showing through. But it is not
only close to us, in front of us, that the divine
presence has revealed itself. It has sprung up so uni-
versally, that we find ourselves so surrounded and
transfixed by it, that there is no room left to fall
down and adore it even within ourselves.

By means of all created things, without exception,
the divine assails us, penetrates us and moulds us. We
imagined it as distant and inaccessible, whereas in
fact we live steeped in its burning layers. *In eo
vivimus.* As Jacob said, awakening from his dream,
the world, this palpable world, which we are wont to
treat with boredom and disrespect, with which we
habitually regard places with no sacred association
for us, is in truth a holy place and we did not know
it. *Venite, adoremus.*

(Teilhard de Chardin, 1975, p. 112)

Because of my love for the world, and my suggestion
that we can find God within it, I have often been called a
pantheist. My first reaction is to say, 'If God is not in all
where is he?' Yet I do know the dangers. It is too easy to
diminish God and confine him to things: to make God
small enough to control or comprehend him. Some people
talk as if they possessed God and could give him to us.
The danger of talking about an immanent God is that we
can trivialize him and forget that we are dealing with the
Almighty. God is greater than all things, even the sum of
all things. He is a transcendent God. God can never be
fully known or fully grasped. Yet what the mind cannot
comprehend the heart can hold. I do believe God is in all
things waiting to be discovered. But because God is

greater than all things, it is far safer to say all things are in God. This makes me a pan-en-theist, which is Greek for believing 'all is in God'. I am an 'entheist' or, to use a very ordinary word, an enthusiast. Believing that all is in God gives life a zest and a depth that so many miss. Become an enthusiast, discover you are in God. Nothing is outside of God and nothing is without God. To discover this is a great homecoming, when we are aware we cease to be strangers and pilgrims, for we have arrived and belong. However, being human, we fail to realize the fullness of this reality. As God is greater than we can ever comprehend, there are always new mysteries and wonders for us to rejoice in. Let us learn to enthuse about the world and ourselves.

A good way of expressing 'we dwell in him and he in us' is to say 'God is in our heart and we are in the heart of God.' Much modern teaching has emphasized that God is in our heart. This is wonderful to know but it can make God like a possession. We need to balance this by saying, 'We are in the heart of God.' From the Hebridean Islands comes a prayer that is a great favourite of mine. It begins by facing the reality of the day, for not every day is wonderful to us humans, and then moves to the wonder of God's care and protection:

> Though the dawn breaks cheerless on this Isle today,
> My spirit walks upon a path of light.
> For I know my greatness,
> Thou hast built me a throne within Thy heart.
> I dwell safely within the circle of Thy care.
> I cannot for a moment fall out of the everlasting arms.
> I am on my way to glory.

> (*Hebridean Altars*, Alistair Maclean, 1937, p. 25.
> Reproduced by permission of Hodder and
> Stoughton Limited)

How wonderful to know that whatever the day we are in the heart of God, protected by him and on the way to glory.

One day I noticed a small group almost skipping along the Pilgrims' Way. They were wearing quite silly hats to express that they were on holiday and out to relax and enjoy themselves. Every now and again, they stopped to look at the birds and to hear their song. I discovered later how they thrilled to hear the seals singing and how they watched them as they cared for their young on a sandbank. In the evening I was privileged to meet this group in church. They were an absolutely radiant group that seemed to spread joy about them. Yet I discovered they were nearly all nurses and working under very difficult circumstances. They spent much of their time dealing with grim and tragic situations.

Their leader came to see me and told me of their joy in walking across the sands, what a freedom it was after a busy city hospital. Like a child she produced a few shells she had collected and said how she would treasure them. She recited with great pleasure the birds she had seen, though she did not know the exact names of all the waders. A heron by a pool had especially brought her great joy. The very delight in her eyes and face made her appear beautiful. She was a pleasure to be with. She told me the group had little knowledge of the Scriptures but a great delight in life. In their work they had learnt a deep respect for the wonder and the mystery of life. Wonder was welling up like a spring from within this nurse: a wonder that could transform desert places like the rock that Moses struck in the desert. I was sure that this little group must have been a great treasure to the hospital and the patients where they worked. As I talked to her I was reminded of words by G. K. Chesterton in his *Autobiography*:

> At the back of our brains, so to speak, there was a forgotten blaze or burst of astonishment at our own existence. The object of the artistic and spiritual life was to dig for this submerged sunrise of wonder, so that a man sitting in a chair might suddenly understand that he was actually alive, and be happy.

They asked me to talk to them about St Aidan and St Cuthbert, though I felt I could have learnt a lot more by listening to them. I presented the two great saints of the Island to them as men with a great enthusiasm for people, for life and for God. The saints live out the reality that heaven and earth are one in God and that nothing separates us from the love of God in Christ Jesus. We had a very lively discussion. The outcome was that we would try to live more enthusiastic lives, revealing we are in God, in his love and his heart.

Exercises

1 Spend some time looking at a single leaf or flower, be aware of its mystery and beauty. The use of a camera or microscope can be a good aid to seeing the flower or leaf without distraction. Know that God created this world and loves it. Rejoice that in him we live and move and have our being. You may like to affirm:

> There is no plant in the ground,
> But is full of His virtue.
> There is no form in the strand,
> But is full of His blessing.

There is no life in the sea,
There is no creature in the river,
There is naught in the firmament,
But proclaims His goodness.

There is no bird on the wing,
There is no star in the sky,
There is nothing beneath the sun,
But proclaims His goodness.

(Carmichael, 1983, pp. 39–41)

2 Read Genesis 28.10–17.

Pause   Unwind in the presence of God. Relax. Let go of all tension. Breathe gently and deeply. Quietly wait upon God, knowing he is with you. To keep the mind at rest you may like to say, 'Surely the Lord is in this place.'

Presence   Know that you do not have to earn God's presence, he is with you. Enjoy being with him. You may like to say:

You Lord are here:
You are in this place,
Your presence fills it
Your presence is love.

Picture   Imagine Jacob at the end of a tiring day. He has left home, possibly in disgrace. He had deceived his father and cheated his brother. No doubt it was no longer comfortable at home. His own brother was planning to kill him. He hoped that he would find some of his relatives to the east and marry one of the daughters of Laban. At the moment he is alone and the future is daunting. Night is near and the darkness will descend quickly. Jacob takes a stone for a pillow and lies down to sleep. Look at his dream with him. See the ladder set between heaven and earth. Heaven and earth are one. Angels are coming and going all the time. God is there. Hear God say: 'Know that I am with you and will keep you wherever you go . . . I will not leave you.' See Jacob awake and over-awed. Life will never be the same again, nor will the world about him. God is with him and in the world. Listen to Jacob as he says: 'Surely the Lord is in this place; and I did not know it . . . How awesome is this place! This is none other than the house of God, and this is the gate of heaven.' Stay with Jacob for a while under the stars and know that you are in Bethel, the House of God.

Ponder It was not under the best of circumstances that Jacob left home. The actual moving away from familiar surroundings and going off on his own may have opened up new sensitivities. Dislocation often makes us more aware. Jacob did not deserve this vision – but God is always gracious. God comes to us, is with us, whether we deserve it or not. Jacob awoke out of sleep; was that a sleep he had been in all his life? There out under the stars his eyes were opened. He saw a greater depth to the world than he had been aware of. Think on the words of Francis Thompson from his poem 'The Kingdom of God':

O world invisible, we view thee,
O world intangible, we touch thee,
O world unknowable, we know thee,
Inapprehensible, we clutch thee.

. . .

The angels keep their ancient places; –
Turn but a stone, and start a wing!
'Tis ye, 'tis your estranged faces,
That miss the many-splendoured thing.

Have your eyes been opened? Do you see beyond the obvious? Can you say, 'Surely the Lord is in this place'? Quietly affirm that, though unseen, God is ever near. Know that God will not leave you or forsake you. That you are in his heart and he dwells in you.

Praise Seek to praise God for his abiding presence each day of your life. Do this at intervals during the day by speaking directly to him. You may like to repeat:

Glory and praise to you Lord God,
You Lord are here:
You are in my heart,
I am in your heart,
Your presence is love.

3 Learn to enthuse about life. Start by taking a single thing that you like and enthuse about it. I still close my Bible up for meditation once or twice a week and instead look at something of God's world in depth,

seeking to give it as much attention as I can. Here is a pattern I based on Genesis 1:

Monday: Explore the beginnings, the Big Bang, the birth of the universe. The balance the world needed for life to evolve. The right amount of gravity, of air, of relationship to the sun.

Tuesday: Discover the beauty and mystery of the sky, the clouds, the air. Again the balance and the ability to recycle water is amazing.

Wednesday: Look at water in all its forms, seas and rivers, ice and snow. Without it nothing would live. Discover how much of the human body is made up of water, or hydrogen and oxygen: the world and ourselves are truly mysterious.

Thursday: Wonder and enthuse over the stars, the sun, the moon, the planets. Explore the balance between the various objects that make up our solar system. Discover how regular are day and night, the tides and the seasons.

Friday: Rejoice in life, in all living things. Look at the wonders of the oceans, the air, the earth. There are many television programmes that help us to appreciate the variety and splendour of life on earth.

Saturday: Enjoy being human. Discover the sacredness of all life. Learn to look at others with awe and respect. Discover our unity of body, mind and spirit.

Sunday: This is a day of rest – make sure you are able to relax. This is the time to enthuse, to affirm you are in the heart of God, and to know in him all things that live and move and have their being.

Practising the Presence

Not everyone needs to travel far on pilgrimage, some will find their holy place in their home or nearby. For some it is not to travel through space but to have a change of heart or mind. For some it is the discovery that God is here: 'His Spirit is with us.' Sometimes our place of pilgrimage can be presented to us by a friend or loved one.

Clare cleaned the church. She was dressed in a plastic raincoat, bright trousers and top, wore sunglasses and a string of beads. She preferred that I chased her to doing the church cleaning! She can be forgiven, for at the time she was hardly three years old. One day I saw her cycling down the street on her 'Barbie' bike. As she was by herself I asked her where she was going. 'I'm going to the pworwy to see Cuthbert.' I knew in an instant she was on her way to the priory ruins to see the new statue of St Cuthbert. On Sundays Clare came to church with her mother and often slept through the sermon; maybe she was not the only one! On weekdays she was brought to church, when it was empty, by her father to 'see the King' and to kneel quietly in his presence. Most days he brought her to the communion rail and let her kneel looking up at the window of Christ's Ascension. Here she was learning to be quiet, to give her love to the King and to stay with him for a while. She would have made a lovely picture as she knelt at the communion rail with her blonde head looking upwards. There she presented herself to her God and was sure that he loved her.

She reminded me of the lady whom Jean-Baptiste Vianney, the Curé d'Ars, found often kneeling in church. When she was asked what she did she replied, 'I look at him and he looks at me.' In his instructions to his people the Curé d'Ars wrote:

> My children reflect that a Christian's treasure is not on earth but in heaven. Therefore our thoughts should turn to where our treasure is. Ours is a noble task: that of prayer and love. To pray and to love, that constitutes the greatest possible happiness for us in this life. Prayer is nothing less than union with God . . . My children I know your hearts are small, but prayer will enlarge them and make them capable of loving God.
>
> (Jean-Baptiste Vianney, quoted in Atwell, 1998, pp. 263–4)

Clare was one of the fortunate ones, her parents were people of faith and wanted their daughter to know and love God. Her father did not come to church services but he wanted to share with her the faith he had learnt. As a father should, he handed on the ability to be still and quiet before God. He sought out times of day when he thought the church would be empty as he preferred the stillness to church services. He would talk to her about the windows and other things in church and then get her to come and kneel for a while before 'the King', telling her of God's love for us and that she should give her love to him.

Every day of the year, we have at least three services in the church. Most are quite formal in that we recite psalms and listen to readings and say a few prayers. We keep a regular rhythm of prayer going throughout each day. Occasionally the service is enriched by a visiting musician or singer but normally it is a said service. One weekday evening service we had just begun the first few words when the door opened. We were used to this as pilgrims often wandered in while we prayed. This time a little voice shouted out quite clearly, 'David, this is for youoo. This is for youoo.' Down the aisle she came repeating the refrain, 'David, this is for youoo. This is for youoo.' We stopped our prayers and watched. The little blonde lass came carrying a large basket of flowers. The congregation of about a dozen were all beaming, if not chuckling. The service was halted. The congregation watched and awaited the presentation. Clare came, looked at me, and said, 'This is for youoo.' Then there was just a slight pause. 'And it is for the King.' She trotted to the sanctuary and placed the flowers at the communion rail. She knelt for a moment in silence. She turned around, gave us a wave and then left, skipping her way out of church. By then, the beaming smiles had turned to watery eyes. With such simplicity and love the little lass reminded us all why we were gathered together and whom we sought. We had also come to kneel before the King and to give ourselves to him. Whatever would be remembered of that service we would not forget the little lass and her flowers.

Clare regularly makes her pilgrimage to see the King and balances her piety by keeping his house clean. She reminded me of the first book I ever read on spirituality. It was *The Practice of the Presence of God* by Brother Lawrence. I had been trying to learn how to meditate and all sorts of wanderings assailed my mind. I wanted to know God in my daily life and not just in church. This book put before me a way that I have continued since, daily conversation with God in my ordinary tasks: 'That we should establish ourselves in a sense of God's Presence, by continually conversing with Him. That it was a shameful thing to quit His conversation to think of trifles and fooleries.'

Brother Lawrence said we should 'practise' the presence of God by talking to him as we went about our daily tasks. God was God not just of the church but of all life. We could talk to him while we swept a floor or washed dishes. We could talk to him as we travelled or as we rested in our homes. I learned from this that God is at home with us and we can be at home with God. God is not fixed in a special place one day a week but is with us always.

I slowly learnt to converse with God, perhaps in the same way as St Patrick mentions in his *Confessions*:

> After I had come to Ireland I daily used to feed cattle, and prayed frequently during the day; the love of God and the fear of Him increased more and more and faith became stronger, and the spirit was stirred; so that in one day I said about a hundred prayers, and in the night nearly the same; so that I used even to remain in the woods and in the mountains; before daylight I used to rise to prayer, through snow, through frost, through rain, and felt no harm; nor was there any slothfulness in me, as I now perceive, because the spirit was then fervent within me.
>
> (*Confessions* ch. 2, in Wright, 1889, p. 53)

I learnt that we can do our daily work rejoicing in God's presence and to his glory. God did not demand that we were in church all the time. When he made Adam and Eve he put them in a garden, in the world, not in a church building. He wanted them to show their love for him in and through his creation. We can do little things for God and for his love. Listen to Brother Lawrence:

> We can do little things for God; I turn the cake that is frying on the pan for love of Him, and that done if there is nothing else to call me, I prostrate myself in worship before Him, Who has given me grace to work; afterwards I rise happier than a king. It is enough for me to pick up a straw from the ground for the love of God.
>
> (*The Spiritual Maxims of Brother Lawrence*, 1906, pp. 34–5)

Not only was I learning to converse with God, I was learning that every act can be done to his glory. If it could not be to his glory it should not be done.

When I went to train with the Society of the Sacred Mission at Kelham near Newark in Nottinghamshire, their motto was *Ad gloriam dei et euis voluntate*, Give glory to God in doing his will. I was soon to discover that I was not only expected to pray and study theology to the glory of God. I was expected to shovel coal, to scrub out urinals, to play football: all to his glory. One wise old monk said to me, 'Remember if you are to clean urinals to the glory of God it means making sure you clean the bits that no one can see!' This was not a religion that would confine me to a building, it opened out all of life and the whole world. I could rejoice in God's creation and give glory to him. I could give him praise through my muscles and my physical actions. I could praise him on a mountain top or in a coal hole. It was not only in the study of the Bible I would find him. I could find him in the study of science or in the study of birds. If we looked close enough and deep enough all things would reveal wonder and awe and lead us to worship. This was the religion of an expanding world and an expanding life. When religion is used to restrict life and adventure we need to look upon it with some suspicion. This was a religion that saw all work as meaningful and that none need be degrading.

The poet Gerard Manley Hopkins wrote:

Turn then, brethren, now and give God glory. You do say grace at meals and thank and praise God for your daily bread, so far so good, but give thanks and praise him now for everything. When a man is in God's grace and free from mortal sin, then everything that he does, so long as there is no sin in it, gives God glory and what does not give him glory has some, however little, sin in it. It is not only prayer that gives God glory but work. Smiting on an anvil, sawing a beam, whitewashing a wall, driving horses, sweeping, scouring, everything gives God some glory if being in his grace you do it as your duty. To go to commun-ion worthily gives God great glory, but to take food in thankfulness and temperance gives him glory too. To lift up the hands in prayer gives God glory, but a man with a dungfork in his hand, a woman with a sloppail, give him glory too. He is so great that all things give him glory if you mean they should. So then my brethren live.

(Taken from an Address based on the opening of 'The Spiritual Exercises of Ignatius Loyola', quoted in Hopkins, 1963, p. 144)

Perhaps my father had a natural inkling of this when I was in my teens. I was asked what I would do as a prospective ordinand. I replied, 'I would seek to give glory to God in all that I do.' In his usual fashion he said, 'Well a good place to start is your bedroom. Go and give it a good tidy up!'

This way of giving glory to God, or better still discovering God's glory in their lives, was the normal pattern for many of the Christians who lived in the Hebridean Islands. They were aware of that presence 'unseen yet ever near'. They would talk to God as they went about their work as naturally as they would talk to a neighbour. Theirs was no remote or church-held God, but a God who went with them fishing or herding their cows. This was a God who was interested in their daily lives, in their joys and in their sorrows. At any moment of the day or night they could turn to him. The eighth-century hymn 'Be Thou My Vision' is a perfect example of this:

> Be Thou my vision, O Lord of my heart,
> be all else but naught to me, save that thou art;
> be thou my best thought in the day and the night,
> both waking and sleeping, thy presence my light.

> Be thou my wisdom, be thou my true word,
> be thou ever with me, and I with thee Lord:
> be thou my great Father, and I thy true son;
> be thou in me dwelling, and I with thee one.

Here is a lovely example of prayer in ordinary situations from the Hebrides:

> When the people of the Isles come out in the morning to their tillage, to their fishing, to their farming, or to any of their various occupations, anywhere, they say a short prayer called 'Ceum na Corach', 'The Path of Right', 'The Just or True Way'. If people feel secure

from being overseen or overheard they croon, or sing, or intone their morning prayer in a pleasing musical manner. If, however, any person, and especially if a stranger, is seen in the way, the people hum the prayer in an inaudible undertone peculiar to themselves, like the soft murmuring of the ever-murmuring sea, or like the far-distant eerie sighing of the wind among the trees, or like the muffled cadence of faraway waters, rising and falling on the fitful wind.

The Path of Right

My walk this day with God,
My walk this day with Christ,
My walk this day with the Spirit,
The Threefold all-kindly.
Ho! ho! ho! the Threefold all-kindly.

My shielding this day from ill,
My shielding this night from harm,
Ho! ho! both my soul and my body,
Be by Father, by Son, by Holy Spirit:
By Father, by Son, by Holy Spirit.

Be the Father shielding me,
Be the Son shielding me,
Be the Spirit shielding me,
As Three and as One:
Ho! ho! ho! as Three and as One.

(Carmichael, 1976, pp. 48–9)

When the transcendent God becomes immanent, when the far-off God comes near, our lives are changed for ever. Into our lives comes a new lightness and joy, as expressed in the 'Ho! ho! ho!' of this prayer. The gravitas has disappeared and there is a levity that is quite uplifting. It reminds me of the saying, 'Angels fly because they do not take themselves too seriously.' When we personally meet God on the road, or when we take off our shoes, or our hat, because we are on holy ground, that place should become for us a lifting place. As we are believers in the resurrection, our encounters with God should be life-enhancing and enriching. We need to take to heart the words of Jesus when he said, 'I came that they may have life, and have it abundantly' (John 10.10). We who believe this must truly want to pass it on to our loved ones and friends, for we cannot keep such good news to ourselves.

One of the sad comments on our time is that our faith is not at home in our homes, our God is not at home in our homes. We have relegated God to the 'holy', to sacred buildings, to services, and so lead most of our lives without him. If our faith, our lives, are to be truly alive we need to have a natural, living relationship with our God in our daily life. Until our faith is expressed in our day-to-day life it will remain weak and lacking in vigour. As our God is with us, we are able to turn to him at all times. We can read how natural this used to be in the Hebrides:

> If we were dilatory in putting on our clothes, and made an excuse for our prayers, my mother would say that God regarded the heart and not speech, the mind and not the manner; and that we might clothe our souls with grace while clothing our bodies with raiment. My mother taught us what we should ask for in prayer, as she heard it from her mother, and as

she again heard it from the one who was before her.

My mother would be asking us to sing our morning songs to God down in the back-house, as Mary's lark was singing up in the clouds, and as Christ's mavis was singing it in yonder tree, giving glory to the God of the creatures for the repose of the night, for the light of day, and for the joy of life. She would tell us that every creature on the earth here below and in the ocean beneath and in the air above was giving glory to the great God of the creatures and the worlds, and the virtues and the blessings, and should we be dumb!

Prayer at Dressing

Bless to me, O God,
My soul and my body;
Bless to me, O God,
My belief and my condition;

Bless to me, O God,
My heart and my speech,
And bless to me, O God,
The handling of my hand;

Strength and busyness of morning,
Habit and temper of modesty,
Force and wisdom of thought,
And Thine own path, O God of virtues,
Till I go to sleep this night;

Thine own path, O God of virtues,
Till I go to sleep this night.

(Carmichael, 1976, pp. 25–7)

Here were people making a short pilgrimage indeed – for they entered the presence as easily as they would come into the presence of their earthly mother or father. As they arose from sleep and put on their clothes, they raised their hearts to God in prayer. We need to capture again the ability to make short pilgrimages, to turn to God in our daily lives and actions. Though this is of the heart, we may need to find a fixed place and a fixed time to get it started. We may have to seek out a special holy place, be it a church or a room in our house, to begin our daily journey into God. If we do not have such a place it is good to create one. Find a quiet place and bring to it a picture or a painting of Christ; I prefer images of the resurrection or ascension. You may like to light a candle or play a piece of reflective music to help you be still. Let this be a place where you 'lift off' for the day. Know that you are not alone, God is with you and offers himself to you.

Once you have found, or made, your holy place, all places become holy. We discover that God is with us in our work and on our journeying. God is with us in our sorrows and in our joys. God is with us in the crowd and when we are on our own. Even in the thick of activity we can quietly talk to him and rejoice that he is there. Do not put off beginning your pilgrimage today, journey closer to God for he comes to you.

Exercises

1 Place yourself quietly before God and say:

> God to enfold me,
> God to surround me,
> God in my speaking,
> God in my thinking.

God in my sleeping,
God in my waking,
God in my watching,
God in my hoping.

God in my life,
God in my lips,
God in my hands,
God in my heart.

God in my sufficing,
God in my slumber,
God in mine ever-living soul,
God in mine eternity.

(Carmichael, 1976, p. 53)

2 Read Isaiah 6.1–8.

Pause Take some time out from your activity and
your busyness. Make a space in your life where God
can be met and known. Learn to let go, to relax. Teach
yourself to be still. Sometimes as I enter a time of stillness I say:

Drop thy still dews of quietness,
till all our strivings cease;
take from our souls the strain and stress,
and let our ordered lives confess
the beauty of thy peace.

Breathe through the heats of our desire
thy coolness and thy balm;
let sense be dumb, let flesh retire;

speak through the earthquake, wind and fire,
O still small voice of calm.

(J. G. Whittier, 1807–92)

Presence   Rejoice that you are not alone, your God is with you. Say:

Lord open my eyes to your presence.
Open my ears to your call
Open my heart to your love.

Picture   Try to feel with Isaiah as he entered the throne room of the Temple. No doubt Isaiah had prayed for the recovery of King Uzziah. But for all the praying Uzziah got worse and died – the throne was empty. The king had been Isaiah's patron, his security, his protection – and the throne was empty. Under the king's care Isaiah flourished and had a future, but now the throne was empty. Isaiah had prayed to God, had hoped, but now the throne was empty. This was an emptiness that filled Isaiah's thoughts and his heart. His future looked bleak and empty. The throne, without the king upon it, symbolized the emptiness of life. Isaiah stood before it in despair. The throne was . . . But then: 'I saw the Lord sitting on a throne.' Suddenly, life and hope arise. Isaiah is not alone, the throne room becomes a holy place, the Lord is here. The day and the world will change from this moment: Isaiah will change. Nothing can be the same, for God is in control. Try to express the difference this must make, 'the whole earth is full of his glory'.

Isaiah's immediate reaction is one of unworthiness. He is a sinful person and he has seen the Lord. How wonderful is the grace of God. He comes to us whether we are worthy or not. God comes to every one of us. We need to open our eyes and our hearts to him. The danger with a vision is that it makes demands. If you are blind to what is going on about you no demands will be made. The test of vision is that it calls us to a higher level and a greater awareness: vision asks for action. Isaiah says: 'Here am I: send me!'

Ponder   How often do we live like Isaiah before his vision? We live as if the throne was empty and God had vacated his world. We rarely turn to God in our daily tasks. We often carry this emptiness within, sometimes we express it by saying we are bored, or by being restless. At other times we seek to fill the emptiness with hyper-activity, with things, with excitement. But nothing will fill the gap that is made for the eternal. Heed again the words of St Augustine of Hippo: 'Lord our hearts are restless until they rest in you.' How often do we sacrifice our peace and our well-being by our refusing to be still before God?

Praise   Praise God each day for the presence and peace he offers to you. Rejoice in that presence and peace, making spaces in your life for God to be able to work in you and through you.

Jesus of the Jelly

A Roman Catholic school came each year from Doncaster, always near Ascension Day. They were a group that would lead the worship and I would speak to them. The teacher who came with them was a gem, making sure the children understood their faith and enjoyed it. The children would read poems, play instruments, sing and lead prayers. They would also sit in absolute silence before a candle or some image they had created to express the love of God. As the church on the Island had the Ascension as the theme for its east window we often talked about the ascended yet ever-present Christ. Above the Christ was a cloud with a stylized sun above it. The sun was hidden by the cloud, yet rays of light penetrated through to the disciples below. Although the symbolism was good, it looked as if the ascended Christ had a large hat above him or a jelly! I loved to describe this window as 'Jesus of the jelly' to get reactions.

One year the Doncaster children were approached this way and asked what they thought of 'Jesus of the jelly'. One little lad's hand shot up and I could see he was bursting to say something. I invited him to make a comment.

Do you not know that it is the Shekinah you are talking about? The sun behind the cloud is about the hidden glory of God. Though we cannot see him God is always present and his glory is all about us. We should all learn about the hidden God who is always with us. This hidden sun represents God our Father and is a very special part of the window.

With this he sat down and puffed out his chest. He had done his job well. There was a beaming smile on the teacher's face and on all of the children's. I knew that I had been set up!

This school group was always well prepared and settled easily into worship. They had discovered something of the glory and grace of God in their lives. For these children prayer and sitting in the presence of God was part of their daily routine at school. It was as vital to them as learning any other subject. In fact their worship often enhanced and enriched the rest of what they were doing and their work enhanced their worship. They were learning that God and his world were not separate and that God could be found through his creation – though he was often well hidden. Even on the cloudiest and darkest days God is still with us.

In *Hebridean Altars*, Alistair Maclean expresses this well:

As the rain hides the stars, as the autumn mist hides the hills, as the clouds veil the blue of the sky, so the dark happenings of my lot hide the shining of Thy face from me. Yet, if I may hold Thy hand in the darkness, it is enough. Since I know that, though I may stumble in my going, Thou dost not fall.

(*Hebridean Altars*, Alistair Maclean, 1937, p. 70.
Reproduced by permission of Hodder and
Stoughton Limited)

The hidden glory of God is always there waiting to be revealed to those who seek it, to those who seek him. As an exercise I have often plunged the church into total darkness as a symbol of our world and our life without the presence of God. If it is in the summer I ask pilgrims to cover their eyes and to keep them completely closed. We remain in the darkness for a while. Then I ask them to open their eyes – look at the light or a lighted candle. The light was there all the time, it was we who had closed our eyes or turned away from it. We had chosen to exclude the light, and now we had turned to the light. If we were suddenly thrust into darkness surely we would strive with all our being to seek the light. In the same way we should seek the hidden glory of our God:

> God who made man that he might seek him – God whom we try to comprehend by the groping of our lives – that self-same God is as pervasive and percep-tible as the atmosphere in which we are bathed. He encompasses us on all sides, like the world itself. What prevents you then, from enfolding him in your arms? Only one thing: your inability *to see him*.
>
> (Teilhard de Chardin, 1975, p. 46)

In a sense that glory will always remain hidden, for God is too great for us to comprehend. Our minds could not contain the full mystery and wonder of God, yet they can forever be excited by glimpses of glory. What the mind cannot grasp the heart can often hold. What we are seeking is not so much intellectual knowledge as a relationship with God: not a collecting of facts but a life-changing relationship. As with all relationships there are always new experiences, new depths, new mys-teries to enjoy and to explore. It is when we lose our relationship with God that our faith becomes dull and struggles.

Moses had a deep relationship with God, his experiences of God's love and care were many, but he was well aware that there was much more to experience, much more to discover of God's glory.

Moses asked, 'Show me your glory I pray.' God's response was

'I will make all my goodness pass before you, and I will proclaim before you the name, "The Lord", and I will be gracious to whom I will be gracious, and will show mercy on whom I will show mercy. But,' he said, 'you cannot see my face; for no one shall see me and live.' And the Lord continued, 'See, there is a place by me where you shall stand on the rock; and while my glory passes by I will put you in a cleft of the rock, and will cover you with my hand until I have passed by; then I will take away my hand, and you shall see my back; but my face shall not be seen.'

(Exodus 33.18–23)

We are always just on the very edge of glory, we get glimpses, but there is much more. The hidden glory is always greater than what we have discovered up to this moment. The exciting thing about this relationship with God is that it is a great adventure that has no end. There are depths beyond depths which we can explore and rejoice in. The Lord is waiting to be revealed to us in each creature, in every life, in every encounter. As Teilhard de Chardin says: 'God truly waits for us in things, unless indeed he advances to meet us'. Though often, like Moses, we are only aware of that glory in hindsight: we only perceive that God has been at work in our lives by looking back over them and seeing where we received guidance or a call that we were not fully aware of at the time.

We will never see all of God's glory but we can strive in this world to gain glimpses of the presence through wonder and awe at his creation. God is always willing to meet us if we come to him. God cannot be captured in words or classified but he will often use words to speak to us. He will come not only in the good and the nice things but in the dark and painful things also. It is for this reason I often turn to the words from *Hebridean Altars*:

When mystery hides Thee from the sight of faith and hope: when pain even turns love to dust: when life is bitter to the taste and our song of joy dies down to silence, then, Father, do for us which is past our power to do for ourselves. Break through our darkness with Thy light. Show us Thyself in Jesus suffering on a Tree, rising from a grave, reigning from a throne, with all power and love for us unchanging. So shall our fear be gone and our feet set upon a radiant path.

(*Hebridean Altars*, Alistair Maclean, 1937, pp. 7–8. Reproduced by permission of Hodder and Stoughton Limited)

Though glory is hidden I am sure there are many ways of discovering it and even teaching that it is there. We need to learn to open our eyes beyond the obvious, to allow our minds to be enraptured by the wonders and mystery of the world, to allow our hearts to be touched by events around us. Many people have lost all sense of wonder and cease to be thrilled by the world about them. Glory is so often obscured totally rather than just waiting to be revealed. I am often reminded of the sad words from William Wordsworth:

There was a time when meadow, grove, and
   stream,
The earth, and every common sight,
To me did seem
Apparelled in celestial light,
The glory and the freshness of a dream.
It is not now as it hath been of yore; –
Turn wheresoe'er I may,
By night or day,
The things which I have seen I now can see no
   more.

The rainbow comes and goes,
And lovely is the rose,
The moon doth with delight
Look around her when the heavens are bare;
Waters on a starry night
Are beautiful and fair;
The sunshine is a glorious birth;
But yet I know, where'er I go,
That there hath passed away a glory from the
   earth.

('Ode. Intimations of Immortality')

As many of the children came from downtown Doncaster, I wondered just how much glory they had in their lives. I am sure it is often well hidden. In many of our cities, and in our lives, there is a feeling that 'there has passed a glory from the earth'. So many live without any recourse to God, without any awe or wonder to really thrill them. So many people feel empty and unfulfilled. It is not that 'glory has departed', rather we have become out of tune with the reality of God. Our eyes have become dulled, as have our other senses. Our hearts are unmoved in dealing with talk about 'God'. Because this higher relationship is missing it affects all our relationships. The Doncaster children were fortunate in having a school that introduced them to a greater vision than what was obvious to them. They were offered the opportunity to see signs of this greater reality throughout their working day and through their relationship with people of faith. In his work *Contra Gentiles* Thomas Aquinas says: 'For a man to be open to divine things he needs tranquillity and peace; now mutual love, more than anything else, removes the obstacles to peace.'

In their growing in the love of God, these young folk were learning that even in the cloud, in the dark day, God was ever present and offering them peace. In a school with a caring and loving atmosphere and with people of vision the children have been able to grow in the faith. They may not be able to see God's presence but they are given the sense he is always there, that nothing can separate them from God and his love. What a contrast between them and the person in the song 'American Pie':

> I went down to the sacred store,
> where I heard the music years before,
> but the man said the music wouldn't play.
> And in the streets the children screamed,
> the lovers cried and the poets dreamed.
> But not a word was spoken
> the church bells were all broken.
> (Don McLean MCA Inc. Mayday Media Arts Music)

Here there was no song or music, the sacred store (the church) no longer had the goods. There was no story being passed on and no relationship offered. Without the deeper relationship people are bereft, there is an emptiness and so children scream, lovers cry and poets can only dream. Without someone handing on the tradition, telling the stories, revealing mysteries and offering relationships, we become impoverished as people and as a nation. Bells no longer ring out in joy if the word is not spoken, and there 'hath passed away a glory from the earth'.

In a world that counts mystery for little and can only live by analysis and classification, we are in danger. Where relationships are counted as dispensable and people can go unloved, communities are in danger of falling apart. We need mystery, we need glory, we need to be able to adore. I was privileged on Holy Island to meet many teachers who were able to bring out deep creativity in their pupils by opening their sensitivities to the wonder, the mystery and the glory that was about them.

At the other end of life, a 91-year-old came upon me one evening at 10.30 pm, as the sun was setting. The swallows had just gone into the church porch for the night and I felt able to lock the door. I would have to open it again by 5 am for the sake of the swallows who were feeding their young. 'Oh, are you locking up?' I said that I was, but it was a moveable feast and could wait. 'I have waited all my life to come here,' he said with tears in his eyes. 'Could I have a few minutes?' I told him he could have as long as he liked as I was in no hurry. If he had waited all his life, I could wait a while. I would stay outside after putting the light on for him. More than ten minutes later he emerged. 'What a glorious place, the whole place is full of his glory.'

I then got the story of his life. He had left England for Australia as a youth and had never returned until now. His young son, in his late sixties, had brought him to the North East where he had been born. As a child he had been told of Holy Island, Aidan and Cuthbert by his parents and his school, but had never visited the place, even though he then lived only twenty miles from it. As time went on, the Island became a symbol for him of the faith he was taught. It was his holy place and he hoped that he might visit it one day. He had a painting of the Island in his bedroom at home in Australia. With tears in his eyes he said, 'It has been well worth it, the church is so full of the glory of God. I was able to kneel before him in the quiet and thank him for all of my life. I have been so blessed to know the love of God and the love of a good family.'

I said a prayer of blessing over him as he stood outside with a backdrop of waves and the Cheviot hills in the distance. Then, before going home, I went back into church for a while and rested in the glory of God, the God who seeks a living relationship with us all.

Exercises

1 Take to heart these words from a spiritual song:

> Oh you gotta get a glory
> In the work you do,
> A Halleluiah chorus
> In the heart of you.
> Paint or tell a story,
> Sing or shovel coal,
> But you gotta get a glory
> Or the job lacks soul.

2 Think over these words by Dag Hammarskjöld and Albert Einstein:

> God does not die on the day when we cease to believe in a personal deity, but we die on the day

when our lives cease to be illuminated by the
steady radiance, renewed daily, of a wonder, the
source of which is beyond all reason.

(Hammarskjöld, 1964, p. 64)

The most beautiful thing we can experience is the
mysterious. It is the source of all true art and
science. He who can no longer wonder or stand
rapt in awe is as good as dead, a snuffed out candle.

(Albert Einstein,
I Believe: Nineteen Personal Philosophies)

3 I like to think on the glory of God using Ignatius
Loyola's 'Contemplation for Achieving Love':

Love consists in a reciprocal inter-change, the
lover handing over and sharing with the beloved
his possessions . . . Recall the good things I have
had from creation . . . See God in his creatures –
in matter, giving them existence,
in plants, giving them life,
in animals, giving them consciousness,
in men, giving them intelligence.
More, he makes me his temple . . .
Think of God energizing, as though he were
actually at work, in every created reality, in the
sky, in matter, in plants, and fruits, and herds and
the like . . .
Realize that all gifts and benefits come from
above . . .

(quoted in Corbishley, 1971, p. 30)

This is a good exercise in discovering the glory and the
love of God – try it!

4 Pray:

> God,
> whose beauty is beyond our imagining,
> and whose power we cannot comprehend:
> show us your glory
> as far as we can grasp it,
> and shield us
> from knowing more than we can bear
> until we look upon you without fear,
> through Jesus Christ.
>
> (Morley, 1992, p. 8)

Pilgrims with Three Legs

Every year there are regular pilgrimages. Americans come from Durham University. Norwegians and Finns come for teaching on Lindisfarne and its saints. Calligraphers come and study the art of the Lindisfarne Gospels. Children come to enjoy a day on the Island, to hear of the heroic deeds of the saints and to learn new ways to pray. There are groups that come each year for teaching and others that come on retreat. Some come for a day or a weekend, a week or even a few weeks. The strangest-sounding group is the one that sometimes says it has three legs and has been walking for twenty-five years! This group is the Northern Cross Pilgrims, who come together for the specific purpose of walking, worshipping and witnessing. They are in fact various groups within a group, who set off from different starting points – a leg being a group that starts from a particular place. One group will start from Haddington in Scotland, another from Hexham in Northumberland, a third may have come from Carlisle in Cumbria – hence three legs. Sometimes there is an additional group of younger children. Starting on Palm Sunday, they will travel from all over the Borders of England and Scotland, each group carrying a large wooden cross. They will go over hill and moorland, through villages and towns carrying the heavy life-sized crosses, walking many miles each day.

It is a spectacular sight to see a group of twenty or so walking up a steep hill carrying a great cross silhouetted against the sky. As they go they sing hymns, psalms and spiritual songs with a few folk-songs and some secular music thrown in for good measure. They have many miles to cover in the week so they must walk an allotted distance each day. This is not for the faint-hearted. The only concession to the group of youngsters is that the cross they carry is smaller and lighter.

In the evenings they will sleep in village or church halls, sometimes giving a performance of a play or some music for the local people. Over the years they have built up a strong relationship with many small communities and have helped to enrich their Holy Week worship. There is a good deal of mutual exchange and all benefit from each other.

By Good Friday the pilgrims will have clocked up many miles and have arrived early in the morning on the western side of the causeway to Holy Island. Because of the Easter full moon, the tides for crossing are always quite amenable. It is here on the shore the 'legs' meet up with great joy as many of the pilgrims have never met before and some have not seen each other since last Easter Day.

The Northern Cross Pilgrims have travelled the sands every Good Friday for around a quarter of a century. The drama continues as the crosses are carried towards the Island. The bare crosses look stark against the open sky and the sands. Services will be held in the church of St Mary and in the Roman Catholic church. Attached to the Roman Catholic church is 'Camp' with dormitories, bunk beds and showers. This is luxury after sleeping in halls and on floors. Many of the pilgrims join in 'The Way of the Cross' at St Mary's, an enactment of the last journey of Christ carrying his cross to his crucifixion. Saturday is mainly a rest day, a day of preparation and practice for the Easter services. Musicians, readers, singers, will all be involved in practising and co-ordinating with each other.

On Saturday evening, along with others, the Northern Cross Pilgrims meet in St Mary's church for the Easter Vigil. We meet in the dark, all lights are extinguished, a symbol of our lives which are often in the dark. It also reminds us of the dark days when Jesus was crucified, dead and buried. The only lights in the church are those used by readers who read the prophecies of God's providing love and care and promising life to his people. We sit in the dark and wait. It often feels like a long time full of promises, promises, promises – but without the light lifting, if anything the dark deepens. We are totally in the dark. One of the extra readings is from Michel Quoist:

Lord, it is dark.

Lord, are you here in my darkness?

Your light has gone out, and so has its reflection on
    men and on all things around me.

Everything seems grey and sombre as when a fog blots
    out the sun and enshrouds the earth.

Everything is an effort, everything is difficult, and I
    am heavy-footed and slow.

Every morning I am overwhelmed at the thought of
    another day.

I long for the end, I yearn for the oblivion of death.

I should like to leave,

    run away,

    flee,

    anywhere, escape.

Escape what?

You, Lord, others, myself, I don't know,
But leave,
Flee.

. . .

It wouldn't matter, except that I am alone.
I am alone.
You have taken me far, Lord; trusting, I followed you,
    and you walked at my side,
And now at night, in the middle of the desert,
    suddenly you have disappeared.
I call, and you do not answer.
I search, and I do not find you.
I have left everything, and now am left alone.
Your absence is my suffering.

Lord, it is dark.
Lord, are you here in my darkness?
Where are you, Lord?
Lord, do you love me still?
Or have I wearied you?
Lord, answer,
Answer!

It is dark.

                              (Quoist, 1963, pp. 107–9)

We all have moments, if not years, of darkness and it is no
use denying it. We have often to struggle against the dark
and against being overwhelmed. There are times when the
Scriptures sound like far-off promises but hardly what is
going on in our lives. With the prophecy from Ezekiel 37
we ask, 'Can these dry bones live?' Like the house of Israel

we say, 'Our bones are dried up, and our hope is lost; we are cut off completely' (37.11). We long and hope for a new day where we can rise and rejoice. We need to hear God and to listen as he says, 'You shall know that I am the Lord, when I open your graves, and bring you up from your graves, O my people. I will put my spirit within you, and you shall live' (37.13, 14). But at the moment we sit in the dark.

After what seems an eternity, we leave the darkened church and go outside. Without light, though because it is Easter there is almost a full moon in the sky, we go down a rocky path. Again this often seems the story of my life, going downhill on a rocky road. If you are not careful it is so easy to stumble and fall. At least there are many fellow pilgrims and we can support each other. One or two timid souls have torches but we mainly walk in the dark. At the front of the group is a large unlit candle.

As we turn the corner we are met with a blaze of light. On the edge of the beach with waves nearby is a bonfire burning brightly. The night is being dispersed, the darkness conquered. As it is on the shore, I always think of Jesus on the shore after his resurrection: 'Just after daybreak, Jesus stood on the beach' (John 21.4). Here we are on the edge, on the shore, of a new world. We have come to rejoice in the presence of the risen Lord. A new day is dawning. We are on the edge of time and eternity. We are on the edge of life and life eternal: on the edge of breakdown and breakthrough. The risen Lord awaits us. Waits to be recognized, invited into our lives and our darkness. Waits for us to come to him. The risen Lord seeks to disperse the darkness that is about us.

When we reach the fire, we stand there for a moment enjoying it. Just being there in its warmth and light. Here are sung words of St Patrick:

Christ, as a light, illumine and guide us.
Christ as a shield, overshadow us.
Christ be before us: Christ be behind us.
Christ be under us: Christ above us.
Christ on our right and on our left.
Christ this day within and about us.
Christ, as a light, illumine and guide us.

Standing before the fire we pray, 'Set us aflame with the fire of your love, and bring us to the radiance of your heavenly glory; through Christ our risen Lord.'

Now for me comes a most difficult act. I am wearing a flowing white robe, an alb, and a loose stole. I approach the fire with caution and feel its searing heat. It will not be the first time I have been singed. Two thoughts pass through my mind, the first from Hebrews 12.28–29, 'Therefore, since we are receiving a kingdom that cannot be shaken, let us give thanks, by which we offer to God an acceptable worship with reverence and awe; for indeed our God is a consuming fire.' In our dealings with our God we need always have reverence and awe, we need approach with care. The second thought backing this up is from *The Lion, the Witch and the Wardrobe* by C. S. Lewis. The lion is called Aslan, and is an image of the Saviour:

'If there is anyone who can appear before Aslan without their knees knocking, they are either braver than most or just silly.'

'Then he isn't safe?' said Lucy.

'Safe?' said Mr Beaver; 'don't you hear what Mrs Beaver tells you? Who said anything about safe? 'Course he isn't safe. But he's good. He's the King, I tell you.'

(Lewis, 1980, p. 75)

Often on the Island the wind is blowing strongly and I have to get downwind of the flames, to avoid the smoke and the searing heat. I attempt to light our large Easter candle directly from the fire. The candle begins to melt and so do I! Suddenly it bursts into flame and I immediately try to protect the light. Sometimes, like our first burning in the faith, the flame is blown out. If this is so, I have to approach the fire again and relight the candle. With the candle burning in the darkness I lift it high and say:

> May the light of Christ, rising in glory,
> banish the darkness, from our hearts,
> from our minds and from this world.

> The light of Christ.
> And all reply *Thanks be to God*.

We came downhill in silence, we now ascend singing joyful songs, such as 'Walk, walk in the Light'. When we enter the church, everyone is given a candle to light. Ideally we would have done this by the bonfire, but the candles would have soon blown out. At the church porch some light their candle from the Easter candle, others light their candle from a friend's candle and so the light is spread around the church. Though some come to faith by a sudden awareness of Christ, most of us receive our faith as handed on to us by one of the faithful. It is good to share the light and to pass it on.

We are all suddenly in a good deal of light. The darkness has gone. You can see faces shining and the light in their eyes. You can see to move around with some safety. The church looks bright and splendid. You can see that it is decked out in splendour for Easter, something we had not noticed while in the dark. Now that we all have the light we proclaim:

The Light of Christ:
Thanks be to God.
Alleluia, Christ is risen:
He is risen indeed. Alleluia.

The rest of the service is one of celebration. We seek to live up to the words of Augustine of Hippo for 'We are Easter people and Alleluia is our song.' This acting out of the drama of the resurrection is fulfilled only if, in Hopkins' words, we 'Let him Easter in us, be a day-spring to the dimness in us.'

After the service the celebration continues with dance and song as we express the joy of the resurrection and the effect it has on us and the world.

The same day, but later in the morning, we have yet another service of rejoicing in a packed church; all seats are taken and many are standing. The Northern Cross Pilgrims will bring in the crosses they have carried across the land. These crosses will now be covered with spring flowers as a sign of new life for us all. With great difficulty they are brought down the central aisle and placed in the sanctuary. They will remain there while we continue our celebrating that death is conquered, we are free, for Christ has won the victory. After the service the crosses are carried out of church and around the village as the pilgrims rejoice in the resurrection and witness to the joy of knowing the risen Lord. In the afternoon and before the tide closes, the crosses will be put away for another year. The pilgrims will go back to their work in towns and cities of our land. But the drama of the resurrection and the presence of the risen Lord will remain with each of us as we go about our daily work and business.

For forty days we will light the Easter candle, every morning and evening. Some will light candles in their home. Each time a candle is lit we will rejoice in the resurrection and say prayers of affirmation and acknowledge the risen Lord. We seek to spend a little of each day, at least, putting ourselves in his presence. Sometimes we will say as we light the candle:

The light of Christ:
Thanks be to God.
Jesus Christ is the Light of the World:
A light no darkness can put out.

We then say a prayer of affirmation like this one from St John Chrysostom (AD 347–407):

Let everyone who loves God rejoice in this festival of light!
With joy we praise our Lord! Alleluia.
Let the faithful servants gladly enter the joy of their Lord!
Our hearts are filled with thanksgiving! Alleluia!
Let those who have borne the burden of fasting come now to celebrate the feast!
We walk from darkness into light! Alleluia!
Let those who were inwardly dead now rise and dance with Christ, the Lord of life!
We are renewed in you, O Christ! Alleluia!

Share this reality with us. Come, each day, and rejoice that 'Death is conquered, we are free, for Christ has won the victory.' Come into the presence of the risen Christ and give thanks that you are alive and that he is with you.

Exercises

1 Rejoice in the risen Lord.

> Discover that through him:
> Goodness is stronger than evil;
> love is stronger than hatred;
> light is stronger than darkness;
> Life is stronger than death.
> Victory is ours through him who loves us,
> Jesus Christ our risen Lord.

2 Read Ezekiel 37.1–14.

Pause   Stop all that you are doing. Too much activity is wearisome. Take a break and learn to be still. Let your body and your mind relax. Allow yourself a little time off. I find that mini-breaks throughout the day make work not only more enjoyable but more productive. Relaxed people usually achieve more. Make sure your whole body is free from tension and your mind from anxiety.

Presence   Rejoice in the presence of God. Let his Spirit flow into you. With every breath remind yourself that God comes to you and is with you. Let God fill your heart and mind. Let go all tension and let God bring you peace.

Picture   Picture the people of Israel, they have lost all hope, they feel dried up as if life had been taken away from them. They have no energy and no motivation, they have entered the valley of dry bones. Look at this 'grave-yard'; lives are lost and wasted for they lack the breath of life. Feel for such people – perhaps you have been there. I have! Now see a change as the Spirit of God moves among them as he moved over creation at the beginning. They come to life, they are filled with Spirit. They will come home and know that the Lord is with them.

Ponder   To be without God is to be in the valley of dry bones. Without God all hope, all human resources, life itself comes to an end. The people of Israel experienced a resurrection, a filling of the Spirit and new hope, new life. Look for moments of resurrection in your life, times of revival and renewal. Do you allow God to refresh and restore you? Maybe you feel you are in the valley of dry bones now. If so, call upon God, 'Lord all our hope is gone, truly our hope is in you.' Do not try to do anything, wait upon God and let God revive you.

Praise   Rejoice each day in the resurrection and in your resurrection:

   I arise today,
   In the power of the Father
   In the peace of the Saviour
   In the presence of the Spirit.

   I arise today,
   To newness of life,
   To refreshment and restoration,
   To live in the eternal.

   I arise today,
   In the love of the Father,
   In the light of the Saviour,
   In the leading of the Spirit.

I arise today,
In the power of Christ's resurrection,
In the joy of his glorious ascension,
In the knowledge of his coming again.

3 Pray:

Today we rejoice in the salvation of the world.
Christ is risen; let us arise with him!
Christ enters new life; let us live in him!
Christ comes forth from the tomb; let us shake off
    the fetters of evil!
The gates of hell are open, the powers of evil are
    overcome!
In Christ a new creation is coming to birth,
Alleluia!
Lord make us new,
Alleluia!

(St Gregory of Nazianzus, *c.* 330–389)

we may even meet dragons

On Being Human

It had been a difficult day. Immediately after the morning services I had to care for a very distressed young woman. She had come to Holy Island for peace and found that it only released demons. She appeared to have no self-esteem at all. During the hour we spent together, I discovered that her father had abused her when she was a child. She had left home and was desperately lonely. Fortunately I was able to put her in touch with someone near her home who could help.

Not long after this I received a phone call to say a woman had just walked off into the sea. By the time I arrived she had walked back out again but was drugged out of her senses. This time it was medical help that was the immediate need and it came quickly. Early in the afternoon I spent some time with a friend who was dying. After the evening service a clergyman approached me; he looked as if he was going to burst a blood vessel. His face was red and the veins were standing out. He said, 'It is all right for the likes of you with a tiny parish and only one church. You could do with a touch of the real world.'

I was tempted to kick him, but did not succumb! Here was someone full of anger and frustration and he needed to take it out on someone. I later discovered he was not satisfied with the room he had been given at the retreat house, nor was he very keen on the others who were staying there. He did not think much of the Island either! This man had come for peace and quiet and was successfully destroying it all around him. He had come away for a change but there was little chance that he was going to get it. In many ways he was like a travelling time bomb that could go off at any moment. He did not need a change of scenery so much as a change of attitude. He needed a change of heart. My mind went to one of the letters of the Stoic philosopher Seneca.

> Here is what Socrates said to someone who was making the same complaint: How can you wonder your travels do you no good, when you carry yourself around with you? You are saddled with the very thing that drove you away. How can novelty of surroundings abroad and becoming acquainted with foreign scenes and cities be of any help? All that dashing about turns out to be quite futile. And if you want to know why all this running away cannot help you, the answer is simply this: you are running away in your own company. You have to lay aside the load on your spirit. Until you do that, nowhere will satisfy you.
>
> (R. Campbell, quoted in Squire, 1973, p. 132)

The clergyman had a load on his spirit and needed to offload it somewhere. I risked staying with him and being a 'punchbag'. I discovered he had a large city parish and very little help. He worked in one of the no-go areas, where all supporting services had been withdrawn. He badly needed human help but was told by his bishop to soldier on! He felt that the authorities were not interested in him or his work. He and his parish had a feeling of neglect and with it a deep anger. Much of the anger was there because no one would listen. I offered to listen, but said I probably could only listen as I was not in the same sort of situation and was unable to offer much advice. He had come to the Island for a break but felt guilty in leaving so many problems behind. I told him I found it hard to say 'No' to pleas for help and that I often found caring for people exhausting. I did not burden him with my troubles of the day or try to justify my existence. We arranged to go for a walk and talk in the evening.

When we met, he almost got back on to the same track. As we walked he said, 'It must be easy to be a holy person in a place like this.' The anger and resentment were still there. I asked him to tell me about his parish and his ministry. As I did a stray thought passed through my mind, 'I bet it is like Argos in Aesop's fable':

> Once Aesop was sitting by the city gate when a visitor asked him, 'What sort of people live in Athens?'
>
> 'Tell me where you come from,' responded Aesop.
>
> 'Oh,' said the traveller scowling, 'I come from Argos – an awful place, full of liars and scoundrels and unfriendly people.'
>
> Aesop spoke with sorrow in his voice, 'I am sorry to tell you, you will find the people of Athens are just the same.'
>
> After a while another traveller came to the gate asking what the people were like in Athens. Aesop once more asked, 'Where do you come from?'
>
> 'Oh,' said the traveller smiling, 'I come from one of the nicest cities in the world. There everyone seeks to be honest and decent, they are so easy to get on with.'

'Friend,' said Aesop, 'I am delighted to tell you that you will find the people of Athens just the same!'

I felt I would be in for a tirade of anger, but it was not like that. The clergyman told me how he loved his parish but how so much of what happened frustrated what he did. He did not want to move away but he wanted a little more understanding. He badly needed someone to listen to him. He talked non-stop as we walked. We sat on a sand dune and watched the sunset as he continued his story. I offered no advice, only a desire to understand as best I could. It was like taking the pressure off a cooker or the cork out of a bottle of bubbly, it was all pouring out of him. At times he was almost in tears; for a while we sat in silence. Suddenly he was aware that he had talked for nearly two hours and he apologized, saying he had better go back to the retreat house. We left it like that, I did not make any comments. But we watched the last rays of the sun in the sky and he said to me, 'Isn't it peaceful.'

The next day he called in the early afternoon, as we had arranged. He said that he had slept better than he had done for weeks. He had been out for a walk with two very nice people who were also staying at the retreat house and had a very relaxing morning. He actually looked like a different person and years younger. This time we sat in my study. As soon as he sat down he tensed up; some memory or hurt obviously flitted through his mind. Thinking it would be less formal, I asked if he would rather walk and talk. He replied, 'No, I am quite happy here.' He didn't look it. Then he saw a postcard propped up on my bookcase; it read 'No problem is too big to run away from.' He actually laughed out loud and asked where I got it. I said I could not remember but he could have it as a gift. He laughed again when I told him, 'I believe what the postcard says but I also know most of my problems run faster than I.' He laughed loudly and said, 'How true.'

Once more he talked for a good while, with me lending an ear and giving him undivided attention. He suddenly stopped, almost in mid-sentence, and said, 'You do not know how good this has been for me. I have got a lot off my mind.' This time, without any aggression, he said to me, 'It must be easy for you to pray in such a holy place.'

It was my turn to laugh. I told a tale I have told more than once. I am fortunate to be able to get the church to myself. I have the key to the door and unlock it before seven in the morning. That normally guarantees me a few minutes or so before the first worshippers arrive for 7.30 am. Picture the church radiant with light. The stillness is awe-inspiring. My pew is near the very spot where Aidan, Cuthbert and many other saints have worshipped. I kneel in this holy place where countless prayers have been said. Then, I think the wickedest thoughts of the week! Prayer will not come and my mind will not behave. Why is this? Because I am human. A holy place does not guarantee holiness or even good thoughts. As a human I am often a battleground and the right and the good do not always win. My prayers are often a struggle. I reminded him that St Cuthbert went to the small island of Inner Farne not for peace but to wrestle with demons.

I took down from the bookcase *Rogue Herries* by Hugh Walpole and read him one of my favourite passages. The setting is just out of Keswick on the road to Watendlath, with beautiful views of Derwent Water and the surrounding hills. All around the scenery is breathtaking. Beauty fills the eye on this road that goes on to Borrowdale. It was here on this road that Rogue Herries met a wandering country preacher called Robert Finch. Herries asked:

'How shall I like this place? It is cut off from the world.' There was an odd note of scorn in the little man's voice as he answered. 'It is the world, sir. Here within these hills, in this space of ground, is all the world. I thought that while I was with Lord Peter-sham all the world was there, but in every village through which I have passed since then I have found the whole world – all anger and vanity and cov-etousness and lust, yes, and all charity, goodness and sweetness of soul. But most of all here in this valley, I have found the whole world . . . You will find every-thing here, sir. God and the devil both walk in these fields.'

I am often very aware that 'God and the devil walk these fields' whether I am in leafy lanes or in the city. I carry this tension within whether I am in a crowd or alone. It is easier to hide from this reality – from myself – in a large crowd or in business. The danger of the country-side and its open spaces or a sudden space and quietness in our lives is that it not only opens us up for God but also for evil. It is for this reason that I am not keen on suggesting to people that they empty their minds. Nature abhors a vacuum, and something will rush into the empty space. I can assure you that if you seek to empty your mind you will soon come up with things you do not want to know – or that you cannot deal with. It is better to take some advice from the writer to the Philippians:

Whatever is true, whatever is honourable, whatever is just, whatever is pure, whatever is pleasing, whatever is commendable, if there is any excellence

and if there is anything worthy of praise, think about
these things . . . and God's peace will be with you.

(Philippians 4.8–9)

The mind is very like a video recorder that is always
switched on: everything you do, everything you have
experienced, everything you have ever thought, all is
recorded in your memory. The problem with this record-
ing is that it is often on random playback, you do not get
out what you want but something else, or when you do
get what you want it often comes with other memories
attached, which may not be good ones. If you want the
mind to play back good memories, it is necessary to put
them in place. The more good memories that are within,
the better chance that they will turn up on random replay.

I would like to take this a stage further. Often people
come to the Island for peace; some are fortunate but
others find they are the same on the Island as they were at
home. I try to persuade such people to give up seeking
peace. Do not look for a present, look for the Presence. In
seeking peace we are like the child playing with the box
and the wrappings while ignoring the real gift. We may get
deep delight from peace, but there is a far greater gift
offered. God offers himself to us. God is willing to walk
with us, to listen to us, to care for us. When God is recognized, when we abide in his presence, we also receive
the gifts we sought. God says: 'My presence will go with
you and I will give you rest' (Exodus 33.14). In this world
the only lasting peace we will find is in his presence.

Rejoice in the Lord always; again I will say, Rejoice.
Let your gentleness be known to everyone. The Lord
is near. Do not worry about anything, but in every-

thing by prayer and supplication with thanksgiving
let your requests be made known to God. And the
peace of God which surpasses all understanding, will
guard your hearts and minds in Christ Jesus.

(Philippians 4.4–7)

Without God all worldly peace is limited and often a
sham. Peace is a gift of the presence of God. Seek not the
gifts but the Giver.

I am aware that most of us have certain triggers that
make us angry. Some of us carry anger around all the
time, and this is very tiring. Sadly the more tired we get
the more prone we are to showing our anger and frustration. A long time ago I learnt that 'rancour produces
torpor', or in plainer English, 'anger makes us perma-
nently tired'. We use up so much energy being angry, or
suppressing our anger, that we do not have enough vitality
to do what we want.

Like the clergyman full of anger, it is often due to the
feeling of being neglected, under-valued, or totally
ignored. Some have carried this feeling from the time they
were infants throughout all their lives. Like so many of
our problems anger is a cry for love, for care, for a
presence. Once we know we are loved and understood
much of our anger disappears.

There are times when it is right to be angry, times when
we should rail against injustice and evil. There is something important missing from our lives if we are not
moved by the greed, the violence, the abuse and the per-
versions that face us in the modern world. I often think on
the words, 'Evil triumphs when good people do nothing'.
Jesus was seen to be angry with the Pharisees who put
their unbending orthodoxy before caring for a suffering
person (Mark 3.1–5). He was angry with the money-

changers in the Temple and drove them out (John 2.13–17). This is an anger that helps to change the world, and it is an anger that is openly expressed. The world would have been denied new freedoms if it were not for the anger of William Wilberforce against the slave trade, and that of Shaftesbury against the working conditions of women and children in the nineteenth century. If it were not for the anger of Martin Luther King at the treatment of coloured people in America, or the anger of Nelson Mandela at the treatment of his people in South Africa, change may not have come about as quickly as it has done. There is a righteous anger which is good and it helps to change situations for the better.

The problem with much of our anger is that it is unspoken and misdirected. The classic example is when we are angered at work: we say nothing and come home and kick the cat! Harboured anger is always a danger to ourselves as well as to others. Anger can be so easily turned into rage which lashes out uncontrollably against anything and anyone. In city riots it is often this sort of rage that is so destructive. William Blake talks of anger as a 'Poison Tree': here are two telling verses:

> I was angry with my friend:
> I told my wrath, my wrath did end.
> I was angry with my foe:
> I told it not, my wrath did grow.
>
> And I water'd it in fears,
> Night and morning with my tears;
> And I sunned it with smiles,
> And with soft deceitful wiles.

St Paul has some good advice about anger. He writes from prison where he must have had to deal with his own anger: 'Be angry but do not sin; do not let the sun go down on your anger, and do not make room for the devil . . . Put away from you all bitterness and wrath and anger . . .' (Ephesians 4.26–27, 31). Be angry – know that it is right to express anger – but do not miss your target. This is the first piece of advice, be angry but do not misdirect your anger. Then 'do not let the sun go down upon your anger'. It is unwise to go to bed angry, it will steal your rest and make you weary. Too many quarrels of yesterday are carried into today. Some groups carry on quarrels that should have been resolved in the time of their ancestors; racial memory of hurts can be dangerous indeed. Modern research has shown that there is danger of adrenalin poisoning, ulcers and head pains: all from carrying around anger. Heed the words, 'do not let the sun go down on your anger'.

The followers of Pythagoras had a rule that if they had been angry with each other during the day, they had to be reconciled before sunset. They must not go to bed harbouring anger against each other. Anger is divisive: the word for the devil in Greek at this point is *diabolos*, 'that which throws apart'. So often we lose our unity, our friendship, even loved ones through unresolved or misdirected anger. Such anger is the cause of dis-ease and disease in our lives.

Paul says get rid of bitterness (*pikria*). This word implies 'long-standing resentment' and unwillingness to be reconciled or to forgive. The danger of past hurts is that we often nurse them to keep them warm, we water them to keep them alive. The more we think upon them the more deep-rooted they become and they take a hold on our time and on our reactions. They do not let us respond to the present or to some people in a new way. Such bitterness can literally turn our lives sour.

With bitterness are outbreaks of passion (*thumos*) and long-lived anger (*orge*). The Greeks recognized such passion as a blazing one which is destructive, as flame would be to a pile of straw. Often it blazes up and then subsides as if it had never been, but it can leave destruction in its wake. Long-lived anger is that which has become part of our being and like a dormant volcano can explode at any time. Long-lived anger often makes us difficult to deal with: it flashes up a sign that says 'Caution, you are walking in a minefield'. How can we hope to be at peace with God if we are not at peace with ourselves or the world about us?

My angry friend would leave the Island with much of his anger abated, but I wondered for how long. He was in a situation that rightly made him angry but where it was hard to vent that anger for there was no single individual at fault. In such a situation he needed a 'soul friend', someone to whom he could turn and express his feelings. I lived too far away to be really useful. I did suggest he could ring me and talk over the telephone but pointed out that he needed a friend close at hand. Too often clergy have been trained to work alone without sharing their needs, their joys and sorrows with anyone. Some clergy have a lot of people around them yet are deeply lonely. From the Rule of Comgall, who founded a monastery at Bangor in the sixth century, we hear: 'Though you think you are very solid it is no good to be your own guide.' Another saying attributed to Comgall is, 'A person without a soul friend is like a person without a head.' As fellow travellers on the road of life, we all need to share our journey, to accept guidance and help as well as give it. Travelling alone is fraught with too many dangers.

Having a soul friend is good for our well-being, for here we are accepted and listened to, here we have someone that cares for us. It is from such friendships that we learn of the love and acceptance of God.

I am pleased to say that the angry clergyman did approach a wise friend who became his soul friend. Much of the pressure was taken away from him by having someone that accepted and understood that the situation caused anger and frustration. Since then he has also befriended a neighbouring clergyman with much the same problems.

Exercises

1 In the silence, picture Christ coming to you and saying 'I am the light of the world'. Now walk with him into your past. Into the dark memories – do not go without Christ! Know that Christ seeks to illuminate the darkness, that he comes to bring love and peace. Put your hand in his and say:

> I walk with you Lord into past pains and hurts and ask your healing.
> Christ come into my past, the remembered and the forgotten:
> Into the room of memories where often anger is stored.
> Come, Christ, with your peace.
> Come into the room of hidden shame,
> Into the room of mourning and sorrow.
> Come, Christ, with your peace.
> Come to where resentment lies hidden,
> Where the mind broods over past offence.

Come, Christ, with your peace.
Come, enter our lives, into our consciousness and
  subconsciousness,
Come to the roots of our personality.
Come, Lord, teach me to forgive
Come, Lord, change me and I shall be changed.

Take your time with this, there is no hurry. Make it a
regular exercise of healing and cleansing.

2 Read Philippians 4.4–8.

Pause   Relax, check over for any anxiety, anger or bitterness that is stopping you enjoying the present. Still
your mind by thinking on what is good and what is joy.
Make sure your body is relaxed, check over each part.

Presence   Rejoice in the Lord, in his presence. Know
that you dwell in him and he in you. Know that nothing
can separate you from his love. In the quiet give thanks
to God for your life and that he is with you. Know that
when God is there, so are all his gifts. God offers his
peace, his love, his forgiveness to you. All of this is for
free, it cannot be earned, it is gratis, it is from God's
grace. Seek God, not his gifts, and you will find what
you need comes with him.

Picture   Imagine two birds, they are hungry, there is
food before them but they cannot eat it for fighting
each other. See how they are destroying each other: how
both are weak with hunger. See yourself using up
energy on wrong pursuits or resentment and hatred. See
how this is preventing you from living your life to the
full. Visualize an improvement in the situation. See the

birds eating together, there is plenty for both of them. Look at areas of your life where you could make similar improvements. It is strange how we often carry anger against some of our own family. Can this be remedied?

Ponder   Think on how you miss the joy of the Lord through being uptight, anxious and un-relaxed. God cannot get to you for the anger and the resentment you carry. If you cannot put them down at least bring them to him. Talk to God about what irks you: talk to him as you would to a friend. Have you got someone you can be open and honest with, someone that you could call a soul friend? Promise to see if you can lay down old resentments, old quarrels, and approach the day with a new freshness: 'let everyone be quick to listen, slow to speak, slow to anger, for your anger does not produce God's righteousness' (James 1.19–20).

Praise

> Praise God.
> Who forgives all your iniquity, who heals all your
>   diseases,
> who redeems your life from the Pit,
> who crowns you with steadfast love and mercy . . .
>
> The Lord is merciful and gracious,
> slow to anger and abounding in steadfast love.
> He will not always accuse, nor will he keep his
>   anger for ever.
> He does not deal with us according to our sins, nor
>   repay us according to our iniquities.
>   (Psalm 103.3–4, 8–10)

3 Here is a prayer I enjoy for its utmost honesty. You may not be able to pray it word-for-word but let it teach you the way to God is through our own situation:

> O God, I am hellishly angry; I think so-and-so is a swine; I am tortured by worry about this or that; I am pretty sure I have missed my chances in life; this or that has left me feeling terribly depressed. But nonetheless here I am like this, feeling both bloody and bloody-minded, and I am going to stay here for ten minutes. You are most unlikely to give me anything. I know that. But I am going to stay for the ten minutes nonetheless.

> (Harry Williams, quoted in
> *The SPCK Book of Christian Prayer*, 1995, p. 191)

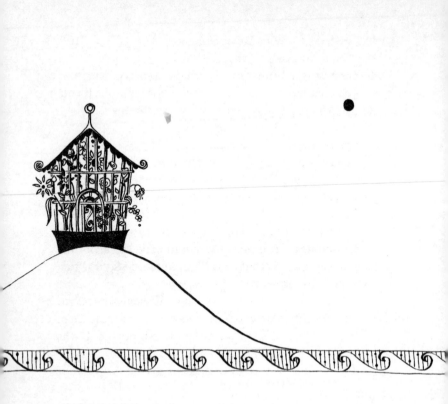

The Cloistered

They had come a long way. They had travelled from the West Country by a hired coach. They had to await the tide opening so I did not expect to see them at the evening service. I was not surprised when they did not turn up for the early morning services either. I was due to meet them for the first time at 10 am and talk on prayer. I was booked for three morning sessions. They were a very pleasant group. At the first meeting I was given their timetable for the full four-and-a-half days they were on the Island. I was a little horrified to say the least. All their time was filled up with speakers, morning, afternoon and evening. I knew the speakers and they would all con-tribute something good but this group would hardly ever leave the building. They were not infirm, they were not immobile but all they did was to be inside. I was politely informed that they would not be appearing at church. I am quite used to this and it did not disturb me but I enquired more deeply. They were used to a certain way of worship and they did not want to change it. They would not even attend the short morning prayers and meditation in the retreat house, because it was not their norm. They were, all in all, very nice people but I could not understand why they had travelled so far. They were not going to look around the Island, or enjoy a change, they were determined that nothing or no one should impinge on their way of thinking or being; even the speakers had been warned not to speak of certain areas.

I am not sure I can really count them among pilgrims. Pilgrims not only change their environment, they seek to bring about change in themselves with new experiences and new awareness. I do believe in the need for retreats, in solitude and in silence. There are times when we need to get away from the daily round that we might get everything in a better perspective. Whenever Jesus was faced with a major change in his life, he sought out a quiet place for prayer and meditation. At the start of his ministry he spent forty days in the wilderness (Matthew 4.1–11). Before choosing his disciples he spent the night praying in the hills (Luke 6.12). After a day spent in healing and speaking and a time of rest, 'In the morning, while it was still very dark, he got up and went out to a deserted place, and there he prayed' (Mark 1.35). When the twelve returned from their mission of proclaiming the gospel and healing, 'He said to them, "Come away to a deserted place all by yourselves and rest a while". For many were coming and going, and they had no leisure even to eat. And they went away in the boat to a deserted place by themselves' (Mark 6.31–32). When Jesus was told of the death of John the Baptist, 'he withdrew from there in a boat to a deserted place by himself' (Matthew 14.13). Crowds sought him out and found him. Once he had dealt with the crowds, 'he went up the mountain by himself to pray. When evening came, he was there alone' (Matthew 14.23). When the final conflict was upon him Jesus went into the garden of Gethsemane to be still before his Father (Matthew 26.36–46). Throughout his life we see Jesus in the thick of activity, then alone at prayer. Whenever he used up energy or faced a major change, he sought to be alone with the Father. It was through his contact with the Father that he was able to turn again to what lay ahead of him.

I value the ability to get away from our normal routine and to be still before God. I have led many retreats where there is a lot of silence and little input from me. I have taught some groups to talk to God rather than to discuss him, though obviously I believe that we need to do both. There have been times when group silence has been strangely vibrant; sometimes the silence of a group seems to create a special kind of silence. There were many times, after a day of hyperactivity, when I would flee to the large beach of the North Shore knowing that I would not meet anyone. Again the words of Columba would come to my mind:

> Alone with none but thee, my God,
> I journey on my way;
> What need I fear if thou art near,
> O King of night and day?

For my days to remain healthy, I needed this silence. For to be renewed in strength I needed to come before my God. It is amazing how a few minutes with our God can so energize us and empower us to return to our daily work. To miss out on this time of quiet is to deny ourselves our birthright as daughters and sons of God. If I am to speak meaningfully about God to others, I need to spend time in his presence and learn of his love. In the same way, if I am to talk meaningfully to God about others and his world, I need to be immersed in the world and relate to others. I rejoice when I hear of groups who have come to be still before God, who will use the beauty and stillness of the Island to draw them in love to their Creator.

Yet this group worried me. There was an awful lot of talking on their agenda, not a lot of silence, not even space to rest or go for a walk. This group would be hyperactive with words. I am always worried by groups that want to talk about God but do not make much effort to talk to him. I felt that they were using dogma to defend their inner uncertainty, using a system of belief to protect them from the world around them. The real world will always challenge our human, dogmatic claims, it will disturb our fantasies and seek to put us in touch with God. But for the rigid in dogma, this is unacceptable, God must approach them through the channels they have chosen or he will be unrecognized. We all live with the danger of a selective egotism that would censor the world, the preacher, the Church, the Bible and even God. We make our belief, our prayers and our God act like a sedative, preventing us from full engagement with the world. It would be better to lose a God that we could grasp and a faith that hid us from our fears, and stand before him with whom we have to do. At some stage we need to discover our God is a consuming fire and is not tameable by us. Our faith should lead us to the borderlands of exploration, to the edge of the unknown, and should encourage us to launch out into the deep. We need to discover that we cannot comprehend God in his fullness, nor can our way of thinking contain God in his entirety. Then we will discover we do not have all the truth, and that we can learn from others and from their approach to God. I have been fortunate on the Island in that I have shared with the Salvation Army, the Roman Catholics, the Methodists and the Greek Orthodox, to mention a few, and I have been enriched by each in their turn. I have entered the church with the incense billowing out, the next time in absolute silence where the worshippers had few words and no actions. Then to a service full of hymns, arm waving and clapping. I have enjoyed many different approaches to God and know he comes to all.

While I talked to the cloistered group I was aware of some very lonely people. It was good that they had come together, yet I felt that they had cloistered themselves in such a way that little could really approach them. I was aware afterwards how they talked but were not listening to each other. They all badly needed to talk – but they were not so willing to listen. It was interesting to look at the questions raised, for few of them related in any way to what I had been talking about. I did wonder if I needed to have been there at all. Later I talked to two of the other speakers and they said that they had a similar experience. This was a group that had travelled many miles but, it would seem, had not moved an inch. After meeting with this group I went home and read from Bonhoeffer's *Life Together*:

> Let him who cannot be alone beware of community . . . Let him who is not in community beware of being alone . . . Each has by itself profound pitfalls and perils. One who wants fellowship without solitude plunges into the void of words and feelings, and one who seeks solitude without fellowship perishes in the abyss of vanity, self-infatuation and despair.
>
> (Bonhoeffer, 1952, pp. 77–8)

It is important that we all know how to deal with silence and being alone. Periods of silence can be enriching, can help to keep us in touch with reality. Albert Camus said, 'To understand the world, it is necessary sometimes to turn away from the world: to serve men better, it is necessary for a moment to keep them at a distance.'

But it is essential that our times of quiet and solitude are enriched by times of encounter and immersion into the world. If we ignore the Presence hidden in the neutron or the nebula, in the stranger or the tramp, we increase our loneliness in a world that teems with his approaches to us. We must not let our limited minds or our timid dogma exclude God, as if we could, or ourselves from the fullness of life. God will not be cloistered. True, he can be found there but he is to be met with in all the world, in our encounters with each other, and within ourselves. Tunnel vision that does not allow us to see what is about us is a great danger to life, it restricts the way we use our eyes, our hearts, our minds. Tunnel vision does not let us see the reality of the present but only what we want to see and is usually concerned more with what has been, what may be, but not about the now. This in turn isolates us and prevents us from making contact with those who come to us. The exciting thing about being alive is that our vision, our experience and our beliefs are all capable of growth and change – and indeed they must if we are to be fully alive. I often use prayers about what the Celts called the 'Five Stringed Harp' – that is, our senses:

> Lord, give me a taste for life in its fullness.
> Lord, fill my eyes with newness and beauty.
> Lord, fill my sense of smell with freshness.
> Lord, give me a sensitivity of touch.
> Lord, open my ears to the call of others and
>   to you.
>
> Then Lord, open my heart, to encounters
>   and love.
> And open my mind to the newness of today.

There is a story from a Celtic monastery that I took to heart years ago. Someone approached the abbess of Clonbroney in Ireland and said: 'I propose to give up study and give myself to prayer.' Abbess Samthann replied: 'What then can steady your mind and prevent it from wandering, if you neglect spiritual study?' Then the monk said: 'I wish to leave and go abroad on pilgrimage.' She replied to him: 'If God cannot be found on this side of the sea, by all means let us journey overseas. But since God is near all who call upon him, we have no need to cross the sea. The kingdom of heaven can be reached from every land.'

It sounds as if this person was in flight from work and study, and had not yet discovered that God is near and heaven within reach.

When Alexander Graham was Bishop of Newcastle, he stood in Holy Island church and said: 'I do not like saying "The Lord is here."' My immediate reaction to this was, 'He is here or he is nowhere.' Yet the bishop and I were in agreement. The bishop did not like saying 'The Lord is here' because it was giving the impression that God was restricted to the church building and the congregation, suggesting a cloistered God. I liked to say 'The Lord is here', because I also said it on the beach, in the crowds at a concert, on a train travelling, when going into a hospital, when looking at a blade of grass under a microscope. I liked saying 'The Lord is here' because it spoke of his abiding presence within the whole world. Heaven can be reached from every place and every encounter.

A group of people who seem to be in direct contrast to the cloistered are the perpetual travellers, and yet they are much the same. One day when the church was very busy I met a young woman peering in from the doorway. 'Is this Holy Island church?' I told her it was and invited her to come and look around. 'Wow, wait until I tell the folk at home I have seen it. Goodbye.' Off she went without ever entering into the building. I felt sorry that she did not have a card to stamp to prove that she had put her nose inside! She belonged to the butterfly world that never stays in one place for long, forever on the move and hardly aware of when they have truly arrived. There is a quotation that applies to such a person's pilgrimage: 'It is better to travel hopefully than to arrive.' Now I love travel but I think only the Tourist Board could really encourage such an idea. We need to know when we have arrived and enjoy being where we are. We need to be able to give ourselves to the present moment and not flit from place to place or thing to thing.

I meet many like this woman. They are collectors of holy places or of ideas and travel ever onward in search of the new. 'We were in Canterbury on Monday, Durham on Tuesday, Holy Island today. We will go to Iona on Thursday and then to Ireland on Saturday. We have a week in Ireland and will visit all the holy places.' How can such people ever get to know a place? They are hardly still enough to get to know themselves. There is a great need to travel in depth as well as distance. As St Augustine of Hippo said:

Men go abroad to wonder
at the height of mountains,
at the huge waves of the sea,
at the long courses of rivers,
at the vast compass of the ocean,
at the circular motion of the stars;
and they pass by themselves without wondering.

(*Confessions*, Book X, Chapter 8)

When I was a child I collected car numbers and filled a book with them. It was a harmless pastime and kept me entertained. I could not see myself spending my life looking for rare numbers. I moved on to collecting quotations and ideas. This appeared to be far more noble – and it is, isn't it? – but we need to have ideas and words that are our own. We should not forever gather crumbs from the wise woman's table when we could bake a loaf of our own. I once saw a hilarious play about an actor who could only speak in roles that he had learned. Even his endearing words of love came from Shakespeare and plays he had been in. This would have been a tragedy except for the loved one that kept catching him out. She loved him for himself and not for the fine words of others. When he spoke in his own words, in a trembling and fearful fashion to begin with, he had a new depth to him. Somehow his own stuttering words said, here you are dealing with reality: he allowed us to see something of himself.

The collectors of holy places could say how some places had touched them. To stand at the place where Jesus was born, or at the Holy Sepulchre, is moving. Yet I suspect though the emotions were moved the heart was often kept in check. We look at it all from a 'safe' distance with a guide who will move us on to the next experience in case we encounter something we cannot control. Yet we are forever brought to the edge of the mysterious, the new and the unfathomable. Borders are usually invisible, we are forever given the opportunity to step out of our cloister, our safety, into a new land and a new encounter with our God. Frontiers are exciting places, and we stand before them each day. We should be encouraged to enjoy them, whether they are the borders of our belief or the edge of a new land. Yet in another way we do need to know when we have arrived. The God whom we seek is waiting for us to stop, to stop running: to know that he is here and with us now.

Exercises

1 Say 'You Lord are here: Your Spirit is with us.'
Say it throughout the day. When you rise, acknowledge the Presence. When you have your breakfast, acknowledge the Presence. When you travel to work,
acknowledge the Presence.

> At work and throughout the day. 'You Lord are
> here:
>   Your Spirit is with us.'
> In joys and sorrows. 'You Lord are here:
>   Your Spirit is with us.'
> In sickness and in health. 'You Lord are here:
>   Your Spirit is with us.'
> When tempted to sin. 'You Lord are here:
>   Your Spirit is with us.'
> In success and in failure. 'You Lord are here:
>   Your Spirit is with us.'
> When out with friends. 'You Lord are here:
>   Your Spirit is with us.'
> In the evening at home. 'You Lord are here:
>   Your Spirit is with us.'
> When you lie down to rest. 'You Lord are here:
>   Your Spirit is with us.'

2 Read Mark 1.16–35.

Pause No need for words, be still and wait to be
recharged, renewed. Check over your body for signs of

tension. Still your mind and keep it from distractions. Enjoy the quiet and that there is no need for action.

Presence   The Lord is always with you. Affirm the presence, say: 'You Lord are here: your Spirit is with us.' This is not a request, this is reality, so seek to be aware that God is with you at all times.

Picture   Imagine a typical day in the ministry of Jesus. Great demands are made of him. Wherever he goes the crowds seek him out. Houses become packed with people seeking him, on the beach or on the mountain-side the crowds follow him. There are times when he feels drained, that power has gone out of him. There is little time for rest. How good it was to be able to sleep. 'Yet, in the morning, while it was still very dark, he got up and went out to a deserted place, and there he prayed.' Picture Jesus moving about quietly, leaving the house for a quiet place. Sleep is important to us. We need sleep to be refreshed for the new day, but Jesus knew that he needed more than sleep to cope with a new day: he needed more than physical refreshment. He needed quietness and communion with the Father. Prayer is an act of love, of contact with the beloved. It is from this meeting that Jesus is ready for what lies ahead and for the crowds that will come. Prayer is often a preparation to face the tasks that are demanded of him.

Ponder   At a time when heavy demands were being made upon him from church and state, Martin Luther had not a spare moment. It was then he wrote: 'I am so busy that I find I cannot do with less than four hours a day in the presence of God.'

Likewise John Wesley put these words on the first page of each of his diaries: 'I resolve . . . 1) to devote an hour every morning and evening to prayer – no pretence, no excuse whatsoever. 2) To converse with God face to face.'

Do we truly seek communion with our God? Has prayer an important place in our lives? Check out how much time you set aside for being alone with God. This may help you to see if God is truly among the priorities of your life. Heed the words of St Jude, verses 20–21: 'But you, beloved, build yourself up on your most holy faith; pray in the Holy Spirit; keep yourself in the love of God.'

Do you see prayer as a way of keeping yourself in the love of God? It is not to make God love you, he does that already, it is to make yourself aware of that abiding love.

It is then you can cope with the activities and demands of the day. Do not forget to stop throughout the day and make regular communications with God, for God is found in all places and with all peoples.

Praise   Praise God, for he is ready to draw near to you if you would but turn to him.

Glory be to you Lord God.
You seek me, before I turn to you.
You call me before I am ready to listen.
Open my eyes to your presence,
Open my ears to your call
Open my heart to your love.
Make me aware of you,
That I may live to your praise and glory

3 Begin the day rejoicing in the Presence: 'This is the day
the Lord has made, I will rejoice and be glad in it.'
Seek to rejoice in God's creation, in your life, in each
encounter:

> May the joy of God go with me,
> wherever life may take me:
> May he bring my desert to blossom:
> May he give me peace in the storm:
> May he fill my heart with love:
> That I may go on my way rejoicing,
> Knowing I dwell in him and he in me.

Life is a Celebration

He came to me out of the mist, as I feared he might! He had dogged my footsteps once or twice during the week but had not approached me. I was just beginning to feel I ought to approach him on a friendly level. He was a sad-looking young man and was droopy in his whole attitude. To make matters worse, he was dressed in black and his face was unusually white. Later I decided that he had used some white make-up. Coming out of the gloom, he reminded me of one of my basic fears, that of becoming a zombie! I had watched lots of horror movies as a child and feared the creature that could come out of the mist and steal away my life, leaving me as one of the living dead. Having lived near Whitby I knew well the story of Dracula. Many people believed it was a true story, perhaps because it reflected how they felt about life. I know the Dracula syndrome, when you awake some morning but life does not rise with you, you get up drained of life and vitality. I did not really believe in Dracula or zombies but I knew the experience of being drained of life. I may be made in the image of God but I was aware that I was also dust of the earth. I had a theory that God created out of chaos and my life, especially my desk top, was trying to return to chaos! There were days when I was aware of my mortality.

When the young man spoke, his question left me trembling. I am not sure now whether I trembled out of fear or laughter. He said, 'Do you believe in life after death?' What can one say as a Christian? Of course I do. I believe that Jesus died and rose for us and in him we have eternal life. But I felt there was a danger of putting off to some future date what should be ours now – life, and life in all its fullness. Too many sad folk project their own desires to a future world when they should be living by faith in this world. I believe in life after death but I also believe in life before death. We need to make sure we are living now. It is for this reason I like prayers that begin with such words as 'I arise today'. Each day is a resurrection day, a day to celebrate our rising to life. Each day we should celebrate the rising to life, not wandering among dry bones of the past but actually celebrating the fact we are alive, that today is new and it brings a freshness to us. When Celtic monks moved away from the monastery where they had spent most of their lives, they usually went to find the place of their resurrection. I do not believe it was just the place where they would die. I am sure it was a place where life was renewed and restored. A place where they freshly experienced the power of the resurrection in their daily lives.

Some days, the future looks bleak and we are full of fears. Then we need to take courage from men and women of the past who have triumphed in the power of God. Joshua struggled at the Jordan and God said to him, 'Be strong and courageous; do not be frightened or dismayed, for the Lord your God is with you wherever you go' (Joshua 1.9). I believe in life before death because I rise in the power of God, I walk in the presence of God. I live in the love and light of God. I am not alone, God is with me. I travel in his strength and due to him alone I shall not perish but have everlasting life. The writer of Deuteronomy has God saying: 'today I have set before you life and death, blessings and curses. Choose life so that you and your descendants may live, loving the Lord your God, obeying him and holding fast to him; for that means life to you and length of days' (Deuteronomy 30.19–20). Choose life and obey God. I see they are options for us and they go together. The choice is ours. We actually need to celebrate and affirm life itself. Every second the world offers us something new, something we have never met before. Every encounter is a chance for new insights, deeper vision. The divine waits to reveal himself to us through what we thought of as common and ordinary. The Christian way is not about diminution but of expansion and newness. Jesus said, 'I came that they may have life, and have it abundantly' (John 10.10). Jesus also says later in St John: 'I have said these things to you that my joy may be in you, and that your joy may be complete' (15.11). Each day we need to affirm the Presence, to remind our hearts and minds and feelings that God is with us. We should celebrate that we are alive and God is with us – if God were not with us we would not exist.

Such a celebration of life stands in direct contrast with the Roman soldier who came before Julius Caesar asking that he might be allowed to commit suicide. He was a wretched, dispirited, lifeless-looking being with no vitality at all. Caesar looked at him and asked, 'Man, were you ever really alive?' Like the soldier, so many people no longer know how to celebrate. They ignore days of celebration and festivity and spend their time trying to create enjoyment. Often they are dispirited, depressed, despairing people filling themselves with drink, activity or things because they feel so empty. Chasing after joy but dragging their sad selves with them. Harvey Cox has said that modern man has been pressed 'so hard towards useful work and rational calculation he has all but forgotten the joy of ecstatic celebration'. Like the people that Ezekiel describes in the valley of dry bones where all hope is gone and they feel dried out and dead. It is the place where they go through the routine and keep up formalities but there is no life. Inside they feel wrung out, empty and inadequate. Without the life-giving spirit this can happen to any of us: it happens to communities, to marriages, to individuals; they plod on but the joy of being alive has fled. This feeling is captured well by Hamlet:

> I have of late – but wherefore I know not – lost all my mirth, forgone all custom of exercises; and indeed it goes so heavily with my disposition that this goodly frame, the earth, seems to me a sterile promontory; this most excellent canopy the air, look you, this brave o'erhanging firmament, this majestical roof fretted with golden fire – why, it appears no other thing to me than a foul and pestilent congregation of vapours. What a piece of work is a man! How noble in reason! how infinite in faculties! in form and moving, how express and admirable! in action, how like an angel! in apprehension, how like a god! the beauty of the world! the paragon of animals! And yet, to me, what is this quintessence of dust?
>
> (*Hamlet*, Act 2, scene 2)

This is not a feeling we are protected from, for we are all a mixture of dust and glory. Some days we awake and are aware that 'dust you are and unto dust thou shall return'. We awake in an awareness that we are perishable beings, that we are mortal – and this is part of our reality. Any who know the heights of our being also experience the depths: any who are aware of the glory given to humans can also feel the humiliation and despair. At least in these feelings we are alive: in our strivings, we are alive. In our struggling and our desire for life, we are alive. If we are not aware of the glory we are not aware of the humiliation either. Only those who have plumbed the depths and scaled the heights are aware that the other is there in their being.

What could I offer that pale-faced young man? He came asking, in his own way, 'What should I do to obtain eternal life?' I could offer him very little, yet God could give him all that he looked for. I could offer him books, words, exercises but I felt that he had plenty of all of these. He needed to know that God was with him, that God loved him and the world about him. That in Jesus Christ God has descended into our hells, our aloneness and emptiness. That the resurrection is a present reality and is happening to us at each and every moment. I offered him my company and sought to say how God was always with him. I suggested a simple daily exercise: First remember that feelings can be liars, they do not always tell us of reality, and can lead us astray. Do not trust feelings alone. Then know we do not rise in our own strength. I cannot cope with the people who say 'Pull yourself together.' We would do this if we could. We cannot lift ourselves by our own shoestrings. We rise in the power and in the strength of God. Hear Jesus say to you each day, 'I say to you arise.' Now seek to give thanks for the earth. I always find it is hard to be miserable and thankful at the same time. I often affirm the presence and love of God by saying:

I arise today by the power of God.
I arise today in the love of the Father.
I arise today in the might of the Saviour.
I arise today in the renewing of the Spirit.
I arise today to the freshness of the earth
To the brightness of the sun
To the glory of light
To the life giving rain:
I arise today.

I was deeply aware that if this young man was clinically depressed he should also seek medical help. In talking to him I felt he needed to learn that he was loved by God and that he was called to love the world as God loves the world.

As I seek to encourage people to celebrate life I am often reminded of the graffiti in the catacombs under Rome, where Christians hid in times of persecution and where it is thought that around six million Christians are buried. This is a shadowy place but the inscriptions in these passages say 'Alive in Jesus', 'Life eternal', 'In peace', or simply 'Life'; the commonest word is 'Life'. The names 'Jesus' and 'Christ' often appear. The Christ does not appear on the cross but is depicted as a splendid young man full of life and vitality. This was not a place of sorrow but of hope. It was a place where they celebrated that life is eternal. I have met so many people that are full of life and rejoice in eternal life. These are not always people that find life easy, nor are they people without their problems and sorrows. They are people that have been given the gift of life: people who celebrate that 'nothing can separate them from the love of God in Christ Jesus'.

I think back to a television programme called 'The Kids from Fame' which was about young folk seeking stardom on the stage. A song they sang often fills my thoughts, 'Life is a celebration'. I see so many seeking to live out these words. I know that 'God turns our mourning into joy' – and I have seen this happen so many times; though on some occasions I have prayed the words of St Teresa of Avila, 'Lord deliver us from sour faced saints.' Sadly, there are still so many Christians who are afraid of life. They look for life beyond death and yet they are too afraid to live now. They need to say 'I believe in life before death.' Surely, if life is eternal we are living it now. It is not only eternal after we die for we are living now and that is part of our eternal life. We are called to live life to the full and to be aware of the fact that in him we live and move and have our being.

To celebrate life does not allow us to escape from the troubles that come along. We will still have our moments of doubt and despair. In fact the higher we rise the further we can fall. If we have a glimpse of glory we can feel greatly bereft when it seems to disappear – but at least we are living in new depths and we are alive. I have often heard people confess their sins, formally or informally. Too often this has sounded like a list of trivial events – but nothing is trivial when it touches our being. Most people do not live in great wickedness but rather below par. They feel they are not up to the mark – and they are quite right. On one glorious occasion a member of a religious community came to me and said he had something terrible to confess, would I hear his formal confession? I said I would.

For a while I heard of what I felt were minor failings common to us all. Then there was a long pause. I knew what was really troubling him was coming next. 'My great problem is, that I find women attractive.' There was a long pause and I waited for more but that was it.

Suddenly with the set words he ended his formal confession. Wow! What could I say, he found women attractive! Here was this holy man kneeling before me struggling with his humanity. I broke all the normal rules of confession and said, 'Join the club, brother! Welcome to the human race!' He looked up at me with wide open eyes and began to laugh. I began to laugh too. We must have looked a strange sight: a monk kneeling at the communion rail and I sitting in the sanctuary and both of us laughing out loud. After a while, and a little silence, I said the formal words of absolution but I made sure that he understood that I did not include his feelings towards women as these were not sinful. I had already ascertained that he was not wanting to have an affair or run off with some woman, he was not lusting after anyone, he just enjoyed the company of women and working with them in the community retreat house. I told him this had its dangers for a religious, but what was the alternative? If he did not like women, he did not like at least half the human race. If he killed his feelings, he was letting something precious die. Surely that we find others attractive is part of our being alive, and part of our celebrating the joy of living.

I have often found more joy and celebration among monks and nuns than I have among young people. Maybe the religious have already struggled with their lives and come to terms with some of their own limitations and failings. They have the benefit of affirming the love and presence of God each day within their community. The lack of community for many of our young people, if not all of us, can make modern living very lonely. In our journeying through life we need companions. I often think upon some words from St John of the Cross: 'The soul that is alone is like a burning coal that is alone. It will grow colder rather than hotter.' To maintain enthusiasm, joy and love we need to be able to express them and share them in community. To celebrate life we need to be with other 'burning coals'.

I have been looking at people as if they were objects – and fixed objects at that – when all are subjects in their own right. They did not come to be studied or to be analysed but to be enjoyed and encountered as living and changing personalities. The way I have looked at them tells you as much about me as it does about them. All of these 'fixed' attitudes have been, can be, part of me and my life. But above all I would like to emphasize that life is ever moving and changing. Even our dogmas are about how far we see at this moment, but we will see further, we will have new experiences and all will change. With our changes in circumstance and mind our dogmas will be found to change also. New experiences bring new vision of life and of our God. The road of life is an adventure and a celebration. We are called to be among the living elements of the world, to rejoice in life and to celebrate our being: to enjoy the fact we live and move, we grow and change, in the presence and power of God.

Sometimes you meet someone you have not seen for years and they say to you 'You haven't changed one bit.' I know it is meant to be complimentary but surely it is an insult to all that we have done and achieved. I know none of the people I have talked about are frozen into a single frame but that all their lives are rich and full of varied experiences. While I have looked at them, many have in the same way looked at me. I have always tried to be open, friendly and available but when you deal with over 140,000 people in a year there are many you must miss or neglect. I have blessed individuals, couples and groups. I have blessed rings, Celtic crosses and icons. I hope that

I have been a blessing as much as I have been blessed. I have tried to give of myself as often as humanly possible for I believe that the gift of ourselves is the finest gift we can offer. This is the gift God asks of us, as well as of those who seek, hope for or demand our attention.

One of the wonderful experiences of the Island is to discover people's capacity to celebrate. Many pilgrimages have been acts of celebration. Some come celebrating a new-found freedom, like the young folk from Slovakia. Couples come to celebrate being married for so many years, or to give thanks for a special anniversary. A few couples come to say a special prayer of thanks for a new phase in their lives together and that old problems are solved. Large groups come and celebrate a saint's day or a special day in the life of their community. Some people come and give thanks for healing, others come seeking it. Some come because of the death of a loved one, or because they have been told their own time is short. Yet they come to celebrate life. Whatever is happening to them, they want to affirm that life is eternal and that nothing can separate them from the love of God in Christ Jesus. I have often been asked, 'Will you celebrate for us?' My reply is nearly always the same, 'I would rather celebrate with you.' How greatly I have been enriched by celebrating with all sorts of pilgrims. I have shared in their dance and in their song. I have travelled a little of their journey with them as we have rejoiced in life.

As I have looked at others for a moment or a day, the words of Robert Burns have often come to my mind:

> O wad some Pow'r the giftie gie us
> To see oursels as others see us!
> It wad frae mony a blunder free us,
> And foolish notion.

> ('To a Louse', written in 1786)

Is it possible to look at anyone without influencing them? If we treat them as objects should we be surprised if they do the same with us? Yet what we see, or they see, is only in part. I ask forgiveness for any who feel they have been subjected to being put under a microscope. Believe me, I do not intend to do that, I have only sought to understand part of the journey and to learn from it. I have seen images of myself at various stages on the road. Not everyone who has met me has found me easy. As a human, I have days when I am tired or weary of visitors. There are times when I have been quite hard on people who want the rewards but not the efforts. Yet I have tried to encourage people to celebrate life and to show young people how exciting and meaningful Christianity is for me.

Because I have looked at others, I would like to end with the image a pilgrim from Vallejo in California captured of me one dark morning. She is called Vicki Gray and her words have often done me the power of good. Though you must realize that with all the people I have met, I was sure to find a few good words about me from at least one of them!

> The church, it's dark.
> I seem alone.
> There's no one else for Morning Prayer.
> Is David away?
> 'Off the Island,' as they're wont to say.
>
> I'll leave, I thought,
> But hesitate.
> I know the words
> I'll pray alone
> this special final day.

But, as I walked
the darkened aisle,
he, too, walked towards me
with his slight
but welcome smile.

My final prayers
were not alone
but offered with this prophet-saint,
my eyes upon the ancient stones
and Celtic knots upon the rug.

The sun now streaming in,
we turned to say 'Goodbye.'
But more was on my heart.
He had changed my life
and had to know.

Some found him stern,
off-putting, others said.
But still they urged me:
'Speak to him
of how you really feel.'

And so, in the morning's gloaming,
I unpeeled my pilgrim heart.
I told him how I felt,
and how he'd set me
on my course.

The tears still come,
as I recall
his inhaled breath,
the twinkle in his eyes.
'Thank you. Journey on,' he smiled.

And so I shall, secure in saintly benediction,
wondering still why he thanked me.

Vicki, I thank you for your generous words and for sharing your pilgrim journey, if only for a short while. In the same way I thank all whom I have met on this pilgrimage of life for every encounter has been an opportunity to be enriched and to meet our God.

Exercises

1 Give praise to God that he is ever with you on the journey of life.

> Blessed are you Creator God,
> To you be praise and glory for ever.
> As your Spirit moved over the waters,
> Bringing light and life to the world,
> So fill us with the same Spirit,
> That we may walk the road of life with confidence,
> Rejoicing in your presence and sharing with each
>   other.
> Blessed be God for ever.

2 In our journeying we need to learn to rest. Think upon the words of Jesus: 'In my Father's house there are many dwelling places' (John 14.2). 'Dwelling places' is from the Greek word *monai*, and suggests staging-posts or resting places on a journey. Jesus tells us that he goes before us to prepare a place for us. We may not know what lies ahead on the road of life but we know who waits to meet us. He offers us rest and, more, he offers himself. He says 'Come to me, all you that are weary

and are carrying heavy burdens, and I will give you rest'
(Matthew 11.28). If we do not accept this invitation we
will find the journey too difficult. Learn to rest on your
journey and make room for God in each day.

I like to use some words of St Augustine of Hippo that
talk of the end of our journey on earth, but I apply
them to each day and try to live by them. Perhaps you
would like to do the same:

> All shall be Amen and Alleluia.
> We shall rest and we shall see.
> We shall see and we shall know.
> We shall know and we shall love.
> We shall love and we shall praise.
> Behold our end, which is no end.

Or you might like to begin the day in the power of his
resurrection:

> I arise today by the power of God.
> I arise today in the love of the Father.
> I arise today in the might of the Saviour.
> I arise today in the renewing of the Spirit.
> I arise today to the freshness of the earth
> To the brightness of the sun,
> To the glory of light
> To the life giving rain:
> I arise today.
> To the journey of life, I arise today.
> To renewal and freshness, I arise today.
> To new encounters and challenges, I arise today.
> To my work and to change, I arise today.
> I arise today by the power of God.

I arise today in the love of the Father.
I arise today in the might of the Saviour.
I arise today in the renewing of the Spirit.

3 Throughout each day seek to give thanks to God. A thankful heart cannot be sad for long, and a thankful life cannot be bored. Joy in living gives us strength for the day. You may like to learn Psalm 103.1–5 and use it regularly:

Bless the Lord, O my soul,
and all that is within me, bless his holy name.
Bless the Lord, O my soul,
and do not forget all his benefits –
who forgives all your iniquity,
who heals all your diseases,
who redeems your life from the Pit,
who crowns you with steadfast love and mercy,
who satisfies you with good as long as you live
so that your youth is renewed like the eagle's.

'Thank you. Journey on.'

References

Adam, D., 1985, *Edge of Glory*, London: SPCK.

Atwell, R. (compiler), 1998, *Celebrating the Saints*, Norwich: Canterbury Press.

Bonhoeffer, D., 1952, *Life Together*, New York: Harper & Row.

Carmichael, A., 1983 (Vol. 1), 1976 (Vol. 3), *Carmina Gadelica*, Edinburgh: Scottish Academic Press.

Corbishley, T., 1971, *The Spirituality of Teilhard de Chardin*, London and Glasgow: Fontana.

Einstein, A., in Auden, W. H. et al., 1968, *I Believe: Nineteen Personal Philosophies*, London: Unwin Books.

Gardner, W. H. (ed.), 1963, *Gerard Manley Hopkins: Poems and Prose*, London: Penguin.

Hammarskjöld, D., 1964, *Markings*, London: Faber & Faber.

Lewis, C. S., 1980, *The Lion, the Witch and the Wardrobe*, London: Lion Books.

Maclean, A., 1937, *Hebridean Altars*, Grant & Murray; repr. London: Hodder & Stoughton, n.d.

McLean, G. R. D., 1961, *Poems of the Western Highlanders*, London: SPCK.

Mayne, M., 1995, *This Sunrise of Wonder*, London: Fount.

Morley, J., 1992, *All Desires Known*, London: SPCK.

Quoist, M., 1963, *Prayers of Life*, Dublin: Gill & Macmillan.

Saint-Exupéry, A. de, 1962, *The Little Prince*, London: Penguin.

The SPCK Book of Christian Prayer, 1995, London: SPCK.

The Spiritual Exercises of St. Ignatius: A Literal Translation and a Contemporary Reading, 1978, St Louis, MO: The Institute of Jesuit Sources.

The Spiritual Maxims of Brother Lawrence, 1906, London: Allenson.

Squire, A., 1973, *Asking the Fathers*, London: SPCK.

Teilhard de Chardin, P., 1975, *Le Milieu Divin*, London: Fontana.

Wright, C. H. H., 1889, *The Writings of Patrick the Apostle of Ireland*, London: Religious Tract Society.